POPULATION DYNAMICS OF SUB-SAHARAN AFRICA

DEMOGRAPHIC CHANGE
IN SUB-SAHARAN AFRICA

DEMOGRAPHIC EFFECTS OF ECONOMIC REVERSALS
IN SUB-SAHARAN AFRICA

EFFECTS OF HEALTH PROGRAMS ON CHILD MORTALITY
IN SUB-SAHARAN AFRICA

FACTORS AFFECTING CONTRACEPTIVE USE
IN SUB-SAHARAN AFRICA

POPULATION DYNAMICS OF KENYA

POPULATION DYNAMICS OF SENEGAL

SOCIAL DYNAMICS OF ADOLESCENT FERTILITY
IN SUB-SAHARAN AFRICA

NOTE: This map, which has been prepared solely for the convenience of readers, does not purport to express political boundaries or relationships. The scale is a composite of several forms of projection.

POPULATION DYNAMICS
OF KENYA

• • • • • • • • • • • • • • • • • •

William Brass and Carole L. Jolly, Editors

Working Group on Kenya

Panel on the Population Dynamics of Sub-Saharan Africa

Committee on Population

Commission on Behavioral and Social Sciences and Education

National Research Council

NATIONAL ACADEMY PRESS
Washington, D.C. 1993

NATIONAL ACADEMY PRESS • 2101 Constitution Avenue, N.W. • Washington, DC 20418

NOTICE: The project that is the subject of this report was approved by the Governing Board of the National Research Council, whose members are drawn from the councils of the National Academy of Sciences, the National Academy of Engineering, and the Institute of Medicine. The members of the committee responsible for the report were chosen for their special competences and with regard for appropriate balance.

This report has been reviewed by a group other than the authors according to procedures approved by a Report Review Committee consisting of members of the National Academy of Sciences, the National Academy of Engineering, and the Institute of Medicine.

The National Academy of Sciences is a private, nonprofit, self-perpetuating society of distinguished scholars engaged in scientific and engineering research, dedicated to the furtherance of science and technology and to their use for the general welfare. Upon the authority of the charter granted to it by the Congress in 1863, the Academy has a mandate that requires it to advise the federal government on scientific and technical matters. Dr. Bruce M. Alberts is president of the National Academy of Sciences.

The National Academy of Engineering was established in 1964, under the charter of the National Academy of Sciences, as a parallel organization of outstanding engineers. It is autonomous in its administration and in the selection of its members, sharing with the National Academy of Sciences the responsibility for advising the federal government. The National Academy of Engineering also sponsors engineering programs aimed at meeting national needs, encourages education and research, and recognizes the superior achievements of engineers. Dr. Robert M. White is president of the National Academy of Engineering.

The Institute of Medicine was established in 1970 by the National Academy of Sciences to secure the services of eminent members of appropriate professions in the examination of policy matters pertaining to the health of the public. The Institute acts under the responsibility given to the National Academy of Sciences by its congressional charter to be an adviser to the federal government and, upon its own initiative, to identify issues of medical care, research, and education. Dr. Kenneth I. Shine is president of the Institute of Medicine.

The National Research Council was organized by the National Academy of Sciences in 1916 to associate the broad community of science and technology with the Academy's purposes of furthering knowledge and advising the federal government. Functioning in accordance with general policies determined by the Academy, the Council has become the principal operating agency of both the National Academy of Sciences and the National Academy of Engineering in providing services to the government, the public, and the scientific and engineering communities. The Council is administered jointly by both Academies and the Institute of Medicine. Dr. Bruce M. Alberts and Dr. Robert M. White are chairman and vice chairman, respectively, of the National Research Council.

Library of Congress Catalog Card No. 93-84968
International Standard Book Number 0-309-04943-1

Additional copies of this report are available from: National Academy Press, 2101 Constitution Ave., N.W., Box 285, Washington, D.C. 20055. Call 800-624-6242 or 202-334-3313 (in the Washington Metropolitan Area).

B167

Printed in the United States of America

WORKING GROUP ON KENYA

WILLIAM BRASS (*Chair*), Centre for Population Studies, London School
    of Hygiene and Tropical Medicine, England
LINDA H. (WERNER) ARCHER, Independent Consultant, Nairobi, Kenya
JOHN KEKOVOLE, Population Studies and Research Institute, University
    of Nairobi, Kenya
SIMON W. NDIRANGU, Ministry of Culture and Social Services,
    Nairobi, Kenya
AINEAH O. OYOO, Nairobi City Commission, Kenya
WARREN ROBINSON, Economic Research Associates, Washington, D.C.

CAROLE L. JOLLY, *Staff Officer*
SUSAN M. COKE, *Senior Project Assistant*
JOAN MONTGOMERY HALFORD, *Senior Project Assistant**

---

*through July 1992

COMMITTEE ON POPULATION

SAMUEL H. PRESTON (*Chair*), Population Studies Center, University of Pennsylvania
JOSE-LUIS BOBADILLA, World Bank, Washington, D.C.
JOHN B. CASTERLINE, Department of Sociology, Brown University
KENNETH H. HILL, Department of Population Dynamics, Johns Hopkins University
DEAN T. JAMISON, School of Public Health, University of California, Los Angeles
ANNE R. PEBLEY, The RAND Corporation, Santa Monica, California
RONALD R. RINDFUSS, Department of Sociology, University of North Carolina, Chapel Hill
T. PAUL SCHULTZ, Department of Economics, Yale University
SUSAN C.M. SCRIMSHAW, School of Public Health, University of California, Los Angeles
BETH J. SOLDO, Department of Demography, Georgetown University
MARTA TIENDA, Population Research Center, University of Chicago
BARBARA BOYLE TORREY, Population Reference Bureau, Washington, D.C.
JAMES TRUSSELL, Office of Population Research, Princeton University
AMY O. TSUI, Carolina Population Center, University of North Carolina, Chapel Hill

LINDA G. MARTIN, *Director*
BARNEY COHEN, *Research Associate*
SUSAN M. COKE, *Senior Project Assistant*
KAREN A. FOOTE, *Research Associate*
DIANE L. GOLDMAN, *Administrative Assistant**
JAMES N. GRIBBLE, *Program Officer*
JOAN MONTGOMERY HALFORD, *Senior Project Assistant***
CAROLE L. JOLLY, *Program Officer*
DOMINIQUE MEEKERS, *Research Associate**
PAULA J. MELVILLE, *Senior Project Assistant*

*through December 1991
**through July 1992

Preface

This report is one in a series of studies that have been carried out under the auspices of the Panel on the Population Dynamics of Sub-Saharan Africa of the National Research Council's Committee on Population. The Research Council has a long history of examining population issues in developing countries. In 1971 it issued the report *Rapid Population Growth: Consequences and Policy Implications*. In 1977, the predecessor Committee on Population and Demography began a major study of levels and trends of fertility and mortality in the developing world that resulted in 13 country reports and 6 reports on demographic methods. Then, in the early 1980s, it undertook a study of the determinants of fertility in the developing world, which resulted in 10 reports. In the mid- and late-1980s, the Committee on Population assessed the economic consequences of population growth and the health consequences of contraceptive use and controlled fertility, among many other activities.

No publication on the demography of sub-Saharan Africa emerged from the early work of the committee, largely because of the paucity of data and the poor quality of what was available. However, censuses, ethnographic studies, and surveys of recent years, such as those under the auspices of the World Fertility Survey and the Demographic and Health Survey Programs, have made available data on the demography of sub-Saharan Africa. The data collection has no doubt been stimulated by the increasing interest of both scholars and policymakers in the demographic development of Africa and the relations between demographic change and socioeconomic developments. In response to this interest, the Committee on Population held a meeting in 1989 to ascertain the feasibility and desirability of a major study of the demography of Africa, and decided to set up a Panel on the Population Dynamics of Sub-Saharan Africa.

The panel, which is chaired by Kenneth Hill and includes members from Africa, Europe, and the United States, met for the first time in February 1990 in Washington, D.C. At that meeting the panel decided to set up six working groups, composed of its own members and other experts on the demography of Africa, to carry out specific studies. Four working groups focused on cross-national studies of substantive issues: the social dynamics of adolescent fertility, factors affecting contraceptive use, the effects on mortality of child survival and general health programs, and the demographic effects of economic reversals. The two other working groups were charged with in-depth studies of Kenya and Senegal, with the objective of studying linkages between demographic variables and between those variables and socioeconomic changes. The panel also decided to publish a volume of papers reviewing levels and trends of fertility, nuptiality, the proximate determinants of fertility, child mortality, adult mortality, internal migration, and international migration, as well as the demographic consequences of the AIDS epidemic.

This report, one of the two in-depth country studies, analyzes the population dynamics of Kenya, with particular emphasis on recent fertility change. Kenya was chosen because of interest in recent survey results indicating substantial demographic change in a country that once had the highest population growth rate in the world. The report examines trends in fertility and mortality and their relationship to socioeconomic changes. As part of this examination, the proximate determinants of fertility are analyzed, and multivariate analysis is used to assess the factors associated with contraceptive use. The report does not examine, in any detail, recent migration patterns because of very limited access to data from the 1989 census.

As is the case for all of the panel's work, this report would not have been possible without the cooperation and assistance of the Demographic and Health Survey (DHS) Program of the Institute for Resource Development/Macro Systems. We are grateful to the DHS staff for responding to our inquiries and facilitating our early access to the survey data.

We are also grateful to the organizations that provided financial support for the work of the panel: the Office of Population and the Africa Bureau of the Agency for International Development, the Andrew W. Mellon Foundation, the William and Flora Hewlett Foundation, and the Rockefeller Foundation. Besides providing funding, the representatives of these organizations, particularly Steven W. Sinding of the Rockefeller Foundation, were a source of information and advice in developing the working group's overall work plan.

This report results from the joint efforts of the working group members and staff and represents a consensus of the members' views on the issues addressed. The Committee on Population and the Panel on the Population Dynamics of Sub-Saharan Africa appreciate the time and energy that all the working group members devoted to the study. The following people deserve recognition for their special contributions: Warren Robinson synthesized a diverse literature on socioeconomic and program factors related to demographic change and drafted Chapters 2 and 6. He also drafted the introduction to the report and was instrumental in guiding the research of the members living in Kenya during the initial stages of the project. Linda H. Archer (formerly Werner) and John Kekovole collected much of the socioeconomic data used to explain recent demographic change and wrote a background paper for the report on socioeconomic changes during the last 20 years. Archer also played a key role in organizing the efforts of the working group members living in Kenya during the later stages of the project. Simon W. Ndirangu and Aineah Oyoo participated in all the working group meetings, and their intimate understanding of the Kenyan experience was useful in drafting the report.

William Brass served admirably as the working group's chair and directed the research of the group. He had primary responsibility for analyzing changes in fertility and mortality and their relationship to socioeconomic change. The results of his efforts are presented in Chapters 3, 4, and 7, which he drafted. Carole Jolly analyzed the proximate determinants of fertility, drafted Chapter 5, and performed the multivariate analysis of the factors associated with contraceptive use, which is presented in Chapter 7. Brass and Jolly served as the principal editors and coordinators of the report. Linda Martin provided substantive comments on numerous drafts of the report and participated in all the group's meetings. Jay Gribble took care of unnumerable details in the final drafting stages. As noted above, however, this report reflects the views of the working group as a whole, and considerable effort by all the members and staff went into its production.

The working group was assisted in its efforts by several other people. Simon Murote Kangethe collected socioeconomic data from numerous Kenyan government agencies. Anne Scott performed data analysis of fertility and mortality trends. Jordan Shapiro authored a paper on migration in Kenya. John Blacker provided extensive analyses of Kenya fertility and mortality, much of which is unpublished.

Special thanks are also due Susan Coke and Joan Montgomery Halford for providing superb administrative and logistical support to the working group, to Florence Poillon for her skillful editing of the report, and to Elaine McGarraugh for meticulous production assistance. Eugenia Grohman was instrumental in guiding the report through the report review process and production.

SAMUEL H. PRESTON, *Chair*
Committee on Population

Contents

Executive Summary

The study of the population dynamics of Kenya was undertaken because of recent survey results that indicated dramatic demographic change during the late 1970s and 1980s. The interest in these changes stemmed from considerable debate about the possibilities for substantial fertility declines in sub-Saharan Africa, a region that has been characterized by longstanding high fertility and child mortality rates. The task of the working group was to examine these recent demographic changes in light of the socioeconomic conditions in Kenya, with the expectation that such a study would provide clues for future changes there as well as in other parts of sub-Saharan Africa. This report highlights fertility and mortality; migration patterns were not examined as part of this study due to lack of recent data.

MORTALITY

Between 1973 and 1984, child mortality fell 27 percent to approximately 110 deaths to children under 5 years of age per 1,000 births. Although mortality had decreased significantly in the 20 years before, this period was notable in that the rate of mortality decline accelerated markedly. The declines were shared almost equally between rural and urban areas, although significant differentials that existed in the 1970s still remain. Mortality differentials among educational groups were reduced, and the large improvement in the mortality rates of children of mothers with no education (a halving between the mid-1950s and the mid-1980s) was particularly noteworthy. Central Province showed the greatest improvements

1

in mortality among all provinces since the 1950s, with a reduction of about 70 percent. Coast Province did rather poorly during the same period, with a decrease of only 19 percent. The four remaining provinces, other than Nairobi, experienced declines closer to the national average of 54 percent.

Attempts to link these trends to socioeconomic factors revealed a strong relationship to female education and adult literacy. Although individual education is probably key in sustaining differentials in mortality over time, evidence from this study indicates the importance of district-wide educational levels in the mortality declines, as demonstrated by the reductions in mortality of children with poorly educated mothers living in districts with relatively highly educated residents. Little association was found between decreases in child mortality and health indicators, although cross-sectional analyses found associations between levels of mortality and the incidence of malaria and malnutrition, as well as the ecological zone of residence.

FERTILITY

Fertility in the 1960s and 1970s was high, about eight births per woman and seemed to be rising slightly. In the decade from the late 1970s to the late 1980s, fertility fell approximately 20 percent to a little more than 6.5 births per woman. This decrease was unexpected by many and was due principally to an increase in contraceptive use. What is striking about the reduction in fertility was its occurrence across almost all subgroups. Declines in fertility occurred within all age groups, with the middle and later reproductive ages contributing more to the reduction than the earlier ages. Other than Western Province (where the evidence for the magnitude of the decline is inconclusive), there were moderate to substantial decreases across all provinces, regardless of level of socioeconomic development. Central Province had the largest decrease of 31 percent.

Fertility fell 17 percent in rural areas, not much less than the 23 percent decline that occurred in urban areas. The reductions by level of education were almost equal in percentage terms, even with marked initial differentials in fertility levels. Decline occurred at all birth orders, a pattern that is clearly distinct from the fertility decline in Latin America and Asia, where fertility reduction began in the middle parities and spread to the higher and then to the lower birth orders. Analysis of other sub-Saharan African countries experiencing changes in fertility indicates that the pattern observed in Kenya is also occurring in Botswana, Nigeria, and Zimbabwe.

The near universality of the decreases in fertility in Kenya indicate that the determinants of the decline have a strong central component affecting geographical and social categories of the population in a similar way although not to the same extent. This conclusion is supported by the weak associations found between the fertility reductions and district-level socioeconomic factors such as education, urbanization, mortality, and population density. The only factor that showed a relationship to fertility decline at the district level was employment (either female or male) in the modern sector.

Given that increase in contraceptive use was the most important proximate cause of the fertility decline, multivariate analysis of the socioeconomic factors associated with use was undertaken. Although the model explained little of the variation in individual-level contraceptive use (which is consistent with the weak associations found at the district level), several important findings were revealed. The number of family planning service delivery points at the district level was found to be the factor most strongly related to individual contraceptive use. District-level and individual-level education had significant effects, as did variables associated with income or exposure to modern ideas—household electricity and type of flooring, membership in a woman's group, listening to the radio weekly, and density of roads within a district. District-level female employment in the modern sector was not significantly related to individual contraceptive use, but it was the most significant factor in determining whether a contraceptor used a modern versus a traditional method. Religion also was not significantly related to contraceptive use, an expected finding given the strong fertility decreases in the Coast Province, which is primarily Muslim, as well as in other provinces where other religions are more prevalent.

THE FUTURE

This study of population dynamics in Kenya suggests several continuing trends for the future of Kenya, in the absence of any marked political or socioeconomic changes. The reductions in child mortality, documented for more than 50 years, suggest that mortality will continue to fall. Because ideal family size dropped from 6.2 children in 1977-1978 to 4.4 children in 1988-1989, it is expected that women will continue to seek to meet this ideal in the next 10 years. The widespread uptake of contraception indicates that the acceptance of family planning has taken hold and will not easily be reversed. Thus, we can expect to see continued demographic change in Kenya, with future declines in fertility and child mortality.

1

Introduction

This report describes the present demographic situation in Kenya, focusing in particular on fertility and mortality, and the socioeconomic factors that are associated with these demographic phenomena. A study of Kenya was undertaken because of the growing evidence that rapid demographic change is occurring there and because of Kenya's success in achieving a high degree of economic and social development relative to other countries in the region. Kenya may very well be a forerunner for sub-Saharan Africa and thus merits special attention.

The report is not a comprehensive, detailed review of earlier research on these topics in Kenya. Nor does it attempt to trace rigorously long-term demographic trends in Kenya. Earlier studies and underlying trends are examined only to set the stage for a closer look at the present and the very recent past. Future trends are dealt with only in a general, probabilistic fashion. Nor are migration patterns analyzed; recent data are not available. The research strategy guiding our analysis is based on very conventional assumptions: namely, that socioeconomic characteristics such as education, material well-being, and the availability of certain public sector social services affect both fertility and mortality. When the vital rates can be shown to be changing, the explanation must be found in some combination of these nondemographic factors. Bongaarts's familiar "proximate determinants" model provides a convenient intermediate framework for analyzing these relationships to fertility and we have employed it. We have also employed multivariate analysis to relate contraceptive practice directly to a selected group of socioeconomic factors.

The report is based, for the most part, on well-known existing data sets, including the several major demographic surveys conducted in Kenya (the Kenya Fertility Survey or KFS in 1977-1978; the Kenya Contraceptive Prevalence Survey or KCPS in 1984; and the Kenya Demographic and Health Survey or KDHS in 1988-1989), the several decennial censuses (1969, 1979, 1989), and various other smaller-scale studies already completed. When the group began work on this report, it was assumed that at least preliminary age-sex breakdowns from the 1989 census would be provided before the work was completed. Regrettably, for various reasons beyond anyone's control, this proved not to be the case, and counts only by highly aggregate units (urban, rural, districts, provinces) were actually available at the time of this writing. This limitation was a setback to the analytical plans originally contemplated by the working group.

Even with this major limitation, the report does say what can be said with any reasonable degree of certainty about the present demographic situation in Kenya and the likely direction and magnitude of future change. It is possible that at some later time, data analysis of the 1989 census data will lead to conclusions different from those reached in the present report, but the working group thinks this highly unlikely. Nor is it likely that another analytical approach would yield fundamentally different conclusions.

The report is organized along straightforward lines. Chapter 2 presents a brief summary of the economic, social, and demographic history of modern Kenya. Chapter 3 examines trends in child and adult mortality in some detail beginning in about 1980. Chapter 4 examines recent fertility changes, also in some detail. Chapter 5 undertakes a proximate determinants analysis of these changes in fertility at the district and province levels, as well as for Kenya as a whole. Chapter 6 examines the policies and programs of the Kenyan government that are likely to have affected the observed changes in fertility and mortality. The public sector family planning program is one such intervention but by no means the only one. Chapter 7 explores the rather striking geographical variation that exists in Kenya in fertility and mortality trends, and attempts to link this variation to differences in socioeconomic characteristics and also to public sector service availability. These results are more illustrative than definitive but seem reasonable in terms of general theory. Chapter 8 outlines the working group's conclusions and takes a brief look at future possibilities.

To repeat what was said at the outset, the working group thinks Kenya may well represent the "leading edge" of future sub-Saharan African demographic developments. Even in the early 1990s, many knowledgeable experts on Kenya argued that traditional, pronatalist cultural patterns were an insurmountable barrier to widespread adoption of contraception in Kenya, and hence to any prospect for declines in fertility. This proved to be wrong. It led to a pessimistic view of Kenya's demographic situation that was unjustified. The working group believes that fertility in Kenya is coming under human control and that, given a continuation of its past economic and social development trends, there is every reason for thinking that a completely viable economic and demographic future awaits Kenya. It also seems legitimate to infer from this cautious optimism for Kenya, equally optimistic if even more cautious, possible outcomes for other sub-Saharan African populations. A "demographic transition" for Africa not only is possible but may well be under way.

2

Demographic and Socioeconomic Background

Kenya has long been considered a "success story" in the developing world and most particularly in Africa (World Bank, 1963, 1975; Parkhurst, 1970; Hazlewood, 1979; Killick, 1981). It has achieved impressive economic gains in the some 30 years of its independent existence as a nation, and it has enjoyed for the most part political stability and social tranquility. But its economic gains have been mitigated in per capita terms by a very rapid rate of population growth. In essence, Kenya's economic growth has been sufficient to allow it to make modest gains in living standards and social welfare in spite of rapid population growth. The country has managed to stay ahead of its population growth, but just barely (World Bank, 1983; Kelley and Nobbe, 1990). Recently, under pressure of both external and internal factors, economic growth has slackened. It appears that population growth has also begun to decrease, but large annual increments to the population will continue for decades to come (Rempel and House, 1978; World Bank, 1983). This chapter reviews the main economic, social, and demographic trends in Kenya since independence in 1963, concentrating on the relatively recent past. Later chapters examine in greater detail the present demographic situation (fertility and mortality) as well as the factors that can be shown to be linked to these recent demographic changes.

By African standards, Kenya is not a large country (Kenya 1989a,b, 1991a,b). Its 569,250 square kilometers rank it twenty-second in size among the nations of sub-Saharan Africa. For administrative purposes, Kenya is divided into seven provinces, with the capital city, Nairobi, also having special status as a province. The provinces are divided into 40 districts that in fact form the primary unit for program purposes, as well as socioeconomic and demographic data collection and analysis (see Chapter 7 and Appendix Tables 7A-1A and 7A-1B for additional socioeconomic information by district). Figure 2-1 shows the provincial and district boundaries of Kenya.

Like many other countries of the region, Kenya's land area is remarkably diverse, with inhospitable deserts in the north, broad semiarid plateaus in the south, and rich, rolling highlands in the center. There are seven main geographic regions: the coastal region, the coastal hinterland and Tana Plains region, the eastern plateau region, the northern plainlands region, the Kenya highlands region, the rift valley region, and the western plateaus region (Nelson, 1983). The coastal region—which includes Kilifi, Kwale, Lamu, and Mombasa plus parts of Garissa, Tana River, and Taita districts— lies along the Indian Ocean. Rainfall is sufficient for agriculture to be practiced in a narrow plain and low plateau area inland from the shore. The southern part is more heavily populated, due partly to better rainfall. Historically, Arab trade flourished along the coast, particularly around Lamu. The coastal hinterland and Tana Plains region, which borders the coastal region, comprises parts of Tana River district and the southern portion of Northeastern Province (parts of Garissa and Wajir districts). There is very little rainfall in this region, and thus, little agriculture, except along the Tana River. Most of the inhabitants are pastoralists.

Moving further inland, one reaches the eastern plateau region, a series of plains comprising the northeastern part of Eastern Province, as well as the southern portion of Rift Valley Province. Rainfall is unpredictable and relatively sparse, particularly in the northern section, which is semidesert. The northern plainlands region covers the northernmost sections of Northeastern, Eastern, and Rift Valley Provinces. It is a very arid region inhabited primarily by nomadic pastoralists, except for some agriculturalists around Mount Marsabit and the base of the Ethiopian foothills, where rainfall is heavier. The Kenya highlands region, which borders the east and west sides of the rift valley in the western and central part of Kenya, is composed of the southwestern portion of Eastern Province, as well as most of Central Province and the western portion of Rift Valley Province. The area, which is characterized by relatively high altitudes, good soil, lower temperatures, and more rainfall, is intensely cultivated and many of Kenya's export crops are grown there.

The rift valley region, lying primarily in the eastern portion of Rift Valley Province, is part of the great rift valley that extends through much of eastern Africa. The population is primarily pastoralist in the northern and southern sections, which receive little rainfall and are semidesert. The central section receives greater rainfall and is suitable for growing grain crops. The western plateaus region, encompassing primarily the Western

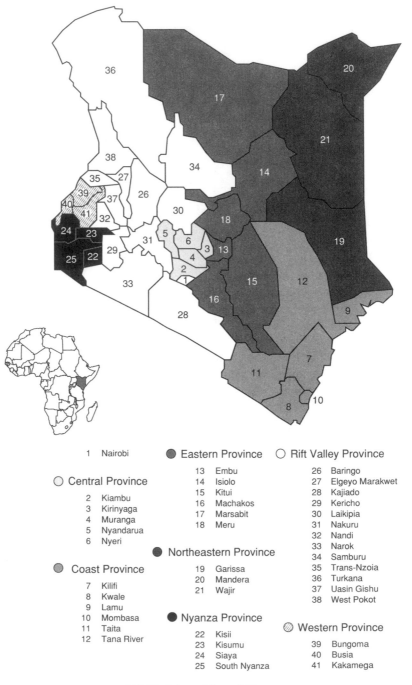

1	Nairobi	● Eastern Province	○ Rift Valley Province

		13	Embu	26	Baringo
○ Central Province		14	Isiolo	27	Elgeyo Marakwet
		15	Kitui	28	Kajiado
2	Kiambu	16	Machakos	29	Kericho
3	Kirinyaga	17	Marsabit	30	Laikipia
4	Muranga	18	Meru	31	Nakuru
5	Nyandarua			32	Nandi
6	Nyeri			33	Narok
		● Northeastern Province		34	Samburu
				35	Trans-Nzoia
◐ Coast Province		19	Garissa	36	Turkana
		20	Mandera	37	Uasin Gishu
7	Kilifi	21	Wajir	38	West Pokot
8	Kwale				
9	Lamu				
10	Mombasa	● Nyanza Province		⊘ Western Province
11	Taita	22	Kisii		
12	Tana River	23	Kisumu	39	Bungoma
		24	Siaya	40	Busia
		25	South Nyanza	41	Kakamega

FIGURE 2-1   Map of Kenya.

and Nyanza Provinces, is mainly a series of plateaus that form part of the Lake Victoria basin. The region is characterized by relatively good soils and sufficient rainfall for agriculture, and thus supports a fairly high population density (Nelson, 1983).

Kenya is still mainly an agricultural country, with some 80 percent of the population living and working on 17 percent of the land. Overall, population density is a low 38 persons per square kilometer, but the rich, high-potential agricultural districts of the west and central regions show densities of 200 to 300 persons per square kilometer. Only about 18 percent of the population lives in urban centers, and more than one-third of the urban population is accounted for by the Nairobi Metropolitan Area. The vast majority of Kenyans are small-scale farmers, but larger-scale farms dominate in the export-oriented sector of agriculture—chiefly coffee, tea, cereals, and livestock products.

Ethnically, Kenya consists of some 70 tribes belonging, for the most part, to the Bantu, Nilotic, Nilo-Hamitic, or Cushitic language groups. The Bantu-related group includes the Kikuyu (the largest single tribal group) and others of the central region as well as the Luhya. The Luo are the largest single Nilotic group and are concentrated in the western region. The smaller tribes making up the other language groups tend to be concentrated in the north, the northeast, and the coastal regions, with smaller enclaves scattered elsewhere in the country.

Kenya is religiously quite diverse, although the majority of Kenyans state that they are Christian. There have been decades of missionary activity, except among nomadic pastoralists in the northernmost regions, and centuries of Islamic influence resulting from trade in the coastal region. Most Kenyans practice a combination of one of these two religions, along with an indigenous religion. Most pastoral groups adhere primarily to indigenous religious beliefs (Nelson, 1983).

SOCIOECONOMIC DEVELOPMENT

Kenya's economic prospects at the time of independence did not appear bright to many observers (Forrester, 1962; Stewart, 1976). Years of domestic unrest verging on civil war had caused considerable damage to an already inadequate infrastructure and had led to an outflow of capital and key technical personnel from some sectors of the economy. The early transition years were halting and uncertain, but the situation soon corrected itself, and by the end of the 1960s the World Bank economic reports were hailing Kenya's "remarkable achievements" and holding it up as a model for other African states. The real growth rate in gross national product (GNP) between 1965 and 1970 was 8.2 percent per annum, the domestic savings rate averaged 15 to 20 percent of gross output, the government budget typically showed a surplus of receipts over expenditures, and the money supply was kept under tight control (World Bank, 1975). These generally cautious, conservative fiscal and monetary policies did not prevent the Kenyan government from launching extensive and ambitious economic and social programs or from pursuing "Kenyanization" of the civil service and of key positions in the private sector. Programs included land redistribution and massive expansion of largely free health and education services focused mainly in rural areas. They were implemented with little or no disruption of previous services, and the gains quickly became apparent to all concerned (Kelley and Nobbe, 1990).

Kenya chose to pursue a market-oriented approach to its development. Economic five-year plans were prepared (and still are), and the state undertook some types of economic activity directly. But private enterprise, local and foreign, was allowed and encouraged to participate in the economy. The government professed a socialist ideal for the nation but carried it no further than occasional rhetoric, a stand that stood in sharp contrast to many of its neighbors who collectivized and nationalized and made war on the private sector. These liberal economic policies undoubtedly helped Kenya in the crucial transition period and also helped fuel her early economic success. This success, as well as the continuing liberal policies, made Kenya attractive to Western aid donors and multinational corporations in the 1970s.

This pattern prevailed throughout the 1970s and 1980s, but with a gradual slowing of the rate of economic growth and a gradual abandonment by the government of the policies that had been responsible for Kenya's early economic success. As shown in Table 2-1, the real growth rate in gross domestic product (GDP) for the 1965-1980 period was nearly 6.0 percent per annum, but for the decade 1980-1990 it fell to roughly 4.0 percent per annum. By the end of this decade and thus far in the 1990s, growth has continued to be modest and is probably negative in the most recent period.

TABLE 2-1 Economic Indicators for Kenya

Economic Indicators	Annual Growth Rate (%)	
	1965-1980	1980-1990
GDP	5.8	4.2
GDP per capita	2.8	−0.3
Agricultural production per capita	1.3	−0.7
Industrial production per capita	6.2	−4.4

SOURCES: Kelley and Nobbe (1990); Kenya (1989b, 1991a,b).

This slowing down has affected both the agricultural and the industrial sectors with the service sector now emerging as the chief source of new employment (World Bank, 1991a).

The driving forces behind this sustained growth in the past were an export-oriented agriculture, tourism, light manufacturing for domestic markets, and Nairobi's emergence as a regional center for clerical and financial services. The public sector has generally avoided direct ownership or operation of productive economic activity. Most utilities and public services were publicly owned at the time of independence and have remained so. Parastatals—publicly owned companies with a private sector-like organization and autonomy from usual governmental administrative and financial controls—have been used to promote particular sectoral or regional development objectives. They have contributed to the slow loss of the early fiscal and financial discipline, but they have not dominated the economy.

Kenya's quite respectable economic growth has not, however, been sufficient to produce any substantial increase in measured output per capita. The present GNP per capita according to the World Bank is about U.S.$370, which ranks Kenya as a low-income country (World Bank, 1992). Per capita income rose by some 2 to 3 percent per annum during the period of most rapid growth but leveled off in the late 1970s and declined in the early 1980s, under the combined effects of stagnating output and continued rapid population growth. Real wages of both public and private sector employees, who comprise the bulk of the modern sector, appear to have fallen sharply in the last decade and now may be only 70 percent of the figure for 1970 (World Bank, 1983, 1991a). Generally, surplus supply in the labor market, lack of unions with any real market power, and a deliberate policy of wage restraint by the government for both the public and the private sectors, to control inflation, seem to explain this trend. What has expanded steadily has been the supply of public services, particularly education, health, and transport and communications infrastructure. The availability of these services is connected with, but not totally dependent on, market-based household or individual income, because these services have been supplied well below cost. Thus, the overall quality of life has probably improved for the bulk of the population (Bates, 1989).

It is difficult to estimate how much of the Kenyan success story has been due to the strong and steady support that was rendered by the international donor community. The World Bank alone has supplied grants and concessionary loans amounting to some U.S.$2.5 billion since 1970 (World Bank, 1991b). Other donors, including the U.S. Agency for International Development, the Overseas Development Administration, the Swedish International Development Authority, and the Finnish International Development Agency, have probably equaled this amount (World Bank, 1991b), and all the major private nongovernmental organizations—Ford Foundation,

Rockefeller Foundation, and others—have also had important roles in Kenya. The relatively open, market-oriented development strategy plus stable, co-operative governments have made it an ideal place for foreign donors to work, and Kenya has certainly benefited. Recent events suggest that this scenario is now being played out in reverse. That is, slowing economic growth and domestic disturbances have led to less liberal, open policies by the government, which in turn have alarmed international donors and caused reductions in the volume of aid, thus increasing economic pressure and further reducing the options open to the government. Success breeds more success, but the same is often true of difficulties.

The economic changes have had a substantial social and perhaps psychological impact in Kenya as well. All sectors and regions of Kenya have become linked to the cash/market economy. The mobility of the population has increased, and modern media reach all groups. Values, perceptions, and attitudes have changed rapidly and continue to change. These ideational changes seem irreversible and are the important link through which the material changes affect demographic behavior, but it is extremely difficult to quantify or measure these relationships.

In a later chapter, we examine at some length those government policies and programs that appear to have had the most direct links to and effects on demographic trends in Kenya during the past 30 years. These have included, in particular, large-scale expansions of the educational and health systems, massive investment in transport and communications infrastructure, and more recently, public sector promotion of family planning.

DEMOGRAPHIC CHANGE

Data Sources

Compared to many sub-Saharan African nations, Kenya is blessed with reasonably good demographic data going back to before independence in 1963 (Henin, 1987; United Nations Fund for Population Activities, 1979). The first conventional census of the population of Kenya took place in 1948. Prior to that, there had been administrative counts. At the 1948 census, ages were recorded only in broad classes and no information on births was collected. However, in each district, certain areas that included approximately 10 percent of the population were selected as representative of the district. For each woman in the selected areas, the total children born to her, the number who died, and the deaths under 1 year of age were recorded.

In the 1962 and 1969 censuses, the detailed information was collected from samples of the population and in all cases these were probability samples. The only questions in the general census were on tribe, sex, and whether the respondent was an adult or a child; the expanded questionnaire collected reports of age in years, births to adult women, and number of living children to adult women. In the 1969 expanded schedule, mothers were asked the number of children born to them now living with them, the number living elsewhere, and the number who had died. Questions on whether mothers and fathers were still alive, for the estimation of adult mortality, were used in a Kenya census for the first time. The information collected at the 1979 census was almost the same as in 1969 but there was no sampling. The general schedule included the questions in the expanded questionnaire of 1969, as well as items on relationships to head of household, sex, age, tribe, birthplace, marital status, education, and residence a year previously. It included questions on whether parents were still alive and, for females aged 12 years or more, details as in 1969 on children born and died. The 1989 census schedule and organization were the same as in 1979, but with an additional question on literacy and a section on economic activity, covering employment in the previous week, main occupation, and work status. There was also a series of items on housing conditions. However, at the time of preparation of this report, only the preliminary counts of numbers by district for 1989 have been released.

The main sources of data on fertility and mortality trends are the censuses and a series of household surveys carried out from the 1970s on. These include several programs that did not cover the entire country, for example, the POPLAB project, an experimental dual-record system for recording vital events, undertaken by the Central Statistical Bureau with financial and technical assistance from the United States from 1973 to 1976, and the Rural Household Budget Survey of 1982. Data from these are not examined here. There were four major country-wide surveys: the National Demographic Survey (NDS) in three rounds, 1977, 1978, and 1983; the Kenya Fertility Survey (KFS) of 1977-1978; the Kenya Contraceptive Prevalence Survey (KCPS) of 1984; and the Kenya Demographic and Health Survey (KDHS) of 1988-1989. All of these projects used the master sample frame of the Central Bureau of Statistics. This frame covers the entire country, with the exception of the three districts of Northeastern Province, Samburu and Turkana in Rift Valley Province, and Isiolo and Marsabit in Eastern Province. Although these are large areas, the population residing there is mainly nomadic and small in number—about 5 percent of the total in 1989 (Kenya National Council for Population and Development, and Institute for Resource Development, 1989). An inspection of the fertility and child mortality measures for these districts, as reported at the earlier censuses, suggests that their omission from the national aggregates of the surveys leads to insignificant biases.

The NDS covered a probability sample of approximately 100,000 persons in both urban and rural areas. The fertility and mortality questions in the NDS were basically identical to those of the 1969 and 1979 censuses.

The KFS covered a sample of 8,100 women. The procedures used were those common to all the countries participating in the World Fertility Survey program (Kenya, 1980). Only female interviewers were used, and they obtained answers directly from the women selected in the sample; proxy answers by their husbands or other members of the household were not accepted. The survey used a detailed questionnaire that was translated into the major tribal languages. The interviewers were thus provided with the exact wording of the questions in contrast to the censuses and the NDS for which they worked from schedules printed in English. The questions on fertility and child mortality were in the form of a detailed birth history that required the date of each birth, the sex of the child, and if applicable, the date of death.

The KCPS of 1984 was a project in the series of investigations in selected developing countries coordinated by Westinghouse Health Systems. The organization and conduct of the fieldwork were undertaken by the Central Bureau of Statistics as part of its National Sample Survey Programme, which also included the NDS and the KFS. The 6,581 women interviewed were asked about births and deaths of children but not about individual detail of dates except for the last born.

The KDHS was a part of the Demographic and Health Survey program (Kenya National Council for Population and Development, and Institute for Resource Development, 1989), which was the successor to the World Fertility Survey. The questionnaires and fieldwork methods of the former evolved from the latter. Essentially the same information on population dynamics was obtained by similar procedures, but there was considerably more detail in the KDHS schedule on contraceptive usage and child health. Completed questionnaires were collected from 7,150 women. Because of the continuity in aims, design, and field methods between the KFS and the KDHS, it is to be expected that comparisons of the two sets of results will not be distorted by operational differences.

Census and Survey Results

Table 2-2 gives the census counts of the population and the intercensal growth rates. There is evidence of differential undercoverage, but it is not adequate for reliable adjustments to be made. The population size from the 1948 census was much larger than the then-current estimate based on the earlier counts updated by an assumed growth rate. How much of the discrepancy was due to undercounts and how much to an erroneous growth rate cannot be determined. It is probable that part of the high growth rate recorded for 1948-1962 was due to the improved completeness of the census, but there is no reason to doubt the rapid expansion of the population recorded from 1962 onward.

TABLE 2-2   Population Size and Growth Rates

| Census Year | Population (thousands) | | | Annual Intercensal Growth Rate (%) |
	Males	Females	Total	
1948	2,680	2,726	5,406	—
1962	4,277	4,359	8,636	3.34
1969	5,482	5,460	10,943	3.38
1979	7,607	7,720	15,327	3.37
1989[a]	NA	NA	21,397	3.34

NOTE: NA = not available.

[a]Provisional.

International migration has made only a small contribution to population growth. The dynamics of change are driven by the balance of births over deaths. The major element that is missing in any attempt to trace this balance over time is a reliable estimate of the course of adult mortality. The measures that have been calculated from the reports of orphanhood at the 1969 and 1979 censuses are restricted in period and uncertain in accuracy. Levels of child mortality and fertility can be determined with fair confidence from the 1950s onward, but with a degree of precision that steadily improves toward the 1970s.

Table 2-3 presents population sizes for 1979 and 1989, plus the intercensal growth rate and population density for each of the districts and provinces of Kenya. Table 2-4 presents estimates of the underlying components of population growth at the national level from 1940 to 1989 in terms of the crude birth and death rates. There is a rising trend in the rate of natural increase (birth rate minus death rate) from the 1940s, reaching a peak in 1975-1979 and declining in the most recent past. The crude death rate declined steadily, but only recently has the crude birth rate begun to do so. The intercensal growth rate and increase in density from 1979 to 1989 reported in Table 2-3 are 3.3 and 40.7 percent, respectively, but the 1989 figures are preliminary and have not been adjusted for underenumeration. Presumably the final, adjusted intercensal growth rate will be somewhat higher. The rate of 3.3 percent for the most recent past—that is, at the end of this intercensal period—would not appear to be too far out of line. In any case, the earlier trend was clear and, thanks to the availability of estimates such as these, this trend became known to Kenyan government policymakers. The first indications of a rising trend in population growth in the 1960s undoubtedly helped spur the adoption of a national population policy and program in 1972. Similarly, the later estimates of natural increase as high as 3.8 percent led to a renewed effort culminating in the creation of the National

TABLE 2-3 Kenya's Current and Recent Past Population

Province/District	Population, 1979 (thousands)	Provisional Population, 1989 (thousands)	Intercensal Growth Rate (%)	Density Per Km^2, 1979	Provisional Density Per Km^2, 1989
Nairobi	828	1,346	4.86	1,211	1,968
Central					
Kiambu	686	914	2.87	280	373
Kirinyaga	291	388	2.88	203	270
Muranga	648	846	2.67	262	342
Nyeri	486	613	2.32	148	187
Nyandarua	233	349	4.04	66	99
Total	2,344	3,110	2.83	178	236
Coast					
Kilifi	431	611	3.49	35	49
Kwale	288	384	2.88	35	47
Lamu	42	57	3.05	6	9
Mombasa	341	467	3.14	1,624	2,224
Taita Taveta	148	202	3.11	9	12
Tana River	92	129	3.38	2	3
Total	1,342	1,850	3.21	16	22
Eastern					
Embu	263	358	3.08	97	132
Isiolo	43	70	4.87	2	3
Kitui	464	640	3.22	16	22
Machakos	1,023	1,393	3.09	72	98
Marsabit	96	125	2.64	1	2
Meru	830	1,138	3.16	84	115
Total	2,719	3,724	3.15	18	24
Northeastern					
Garissa	129	124	-0.40	3	3
Mandera	106	123	1.49	4	5
Wajir	139	125	-1.06	2	2
Total	374	372	-0.05	3	3

Nyanza					
Kisii	870	1,146	2.76	396	522
Kisumu	482	674	3.35	232	324
Siaya	475	643	3.03	187	254
South Nyanza	818	1,095	2.92	143	192
Total	2,645	3,558	2.97	211	284
Rift Valley					
Kajiado	149	262	5.64	6	10
Kericho	633	859	3.05	107	176
Laikipia	135	213	4.56	31	45
Nakuru	523	862	5.00	30	57
Nandi	299	440	3.86	74	104
Narok	210	402	6.49	8	11
Baringo	204	286	3.38	14	25
Elgeyo Marakwet	149	212	3.53	233	316
Samburu	77	114	3.92	4	5
Trans-Nzoia	260	394	4.16	105	160
Turkana	143	179	2.25	2	3
Uasin Gishu	301	440	3.80	80	116
West Pokot	159	231	3.74	31	46
Total	3,242	4,894	4.12	19	29
Western					
Bungoma	504	731	3.72	164	238
Busia	298	423	3.50	183	260
Kakamega	1,031	1,389	2.98	293	395
Total	1,833	2,543	3.27	223	309
National total	15,327	21,397	3.34	27	38

SOURCE: Kenya (1991a).

TABLE 2-4   Vital Rates per 1,000 Population

Period	Crude Birth Rate	Crude Death Rate	Natural Increase
ca.1940[a]	40	25	15
1958-1962[a]	48	20	28
1965-1969[a]	50	17	33
1975-1979[a]	52	14	38
1985-1989[b]	45	11	34

[a]Approximate estimates from census data for recent preceding period.
[b]Provisional estimates from KDHS.

Council on Population and Development, and numerous new initiatives in the 1980s. Better data and analysis influenced policy and program development in Kenya in a nearly textbook fashion.

Table 2-5 examines more closely the underlying vital processes of fertility and mortality. The total fertility rates (TFRs) shown in Table 2-5 suggest an increase from before the 1960s to the 1970s, after which fertility plateaued and then began falling in the 1980s. There is some doubt about this early upward movement, however. A detailed, unpublished examination of fertility in Kenya, undertaken in the early 1980s, concluded that fertility had been essentially constant for the previous 15 to 20 years at a TFR of roughly 8.0 children per woman (Panel on Tropical Africa, 1981). The apparent increase, this study argued, was due to the improved accuracy of data. On the other hand, the study did find evidence of slight increases in fertility in some regions, notably the coast, as well as slight declines in others, and therefore, slight changes in the overall TFR could not be totally ruled out. An increase would, moreover, be consistent with increases in

TABLE 2-5   Measures of Fertility and Mortality

Period	Total Fertility Rate	Probability of Dying by Age 5 (per 1,000)	Life Expectancy at Birth (years)
ca. 1940[a]	5.5	270	37
1958-1962[a]	7.0	220	43
1965-1969[a]	7.6	190	49
1975-1979[a]	7.9	150	54
1985-1989[b]	6.7	110	NA

NOTE: NA = not available.

[a]Approximate estimates from census data for recent preceding period.
[b]Provisional estimates from KDHS.

nutrition and prenatal health care, and reduced fetal mortality, all of which were presumably occurring during this period. These changes in fertility 20 years ago are mainly of academic interest, however, since they seem to have little bearing on present or future trends.

Fertility began to fall in the 1980s. The 1984 KCPS gave an indication of this change with a reported TFR of 7.7 compared to previous estimates of close to 8.0. The 1984 data showed that contraceptive attitudes, knowledge, and practice were also in the process of change. The 1989 KDHS made clear that these changes continued and accelerated in the most recent past, which surprised many knowledgeable observers. The apparent constancy or even increases of fertility in the earlier data had led to a conventional wisdom that fertility in Kenya was high and would remain high (Frank and McNicoll, 1987). This point of view saw Kenya, and most of sub-Saharan Africa, as being staunchly pronatalist and anti-family planning, and unlikely to change for years to come. The recent data from Kenya being considered here would seem to provide a refutation of this argument (Robinson, 1992). This recent evidence, and the KDHS in particular, are considered at length in Chapter 4.

Let us turn now to the mortality trends shown in Table 2-5. The child mortality rate has fallen by 50 percent in the last 30 years, and expectation of life at birth has increased by roughly one-third. These trends are reflected, as we have seen, in the steady decline in the crude death rate (Table 2-4). Even if one accepts that fertility may have risen slightly in the past, it has clearly been this rapid, sustained decline in mortality that has generated the explosive growth rates of the Kenyan population in the last several decades. In sum, Kenya has undergone the first phase of a classic demographic transition, declining mortality coupled with relatively constant fertility. This phase would now appear to be complete, because future mortality declines will be more modest and therefore not affect the overall growth rate as much. Fertility is now the crucial process governing growth.

It is important to include here information on the trends in the contraceptive prevalence rate over this longer-term period. Table 2-6 presents the relevant data for the three most recent surveys, which cover some 15 years. In 1988-1989, 27 percent of married women in Kenya were using a contraceptive method, compared to 17 percent in 1984 and 6 percent in 1977-1978. Contraceptive prevalence increased almost fourfold over 12 years. The KDHS showed a shift from traditional toward modern methods of contraception. Nearly all of the increase between 1984 and 1989 was in the use of modern methods, which now account for two-thirds of all use.

The other indicators of knowledge and attitudes about family planning also showed considerable change over the 12-year period. In 1988-1989, 40 percent of all women reported having ever used contraception, compared to 30 percent in 1984. Almost 90 percent were familiar with at least one

TABLE 2-6   Indicators of Family Planning Knowledge, Attitude, and
Practice in Kenya

Indicators	1977-1978 KFS	1984 KCPS	1988-1989 KDHS
Current use of any method (%)[a]	5.6	17.0	27.0
Current use of modern methods (%)[a]	4.3	9.0	18.0
Ever use of any method (%)[b]	29.0	29.0	39.0
Knows any method (%)[b]	81.0	88.0	90.0
Knows a modern method (%)[b]	84.0	83.0	88.4
Currently pregnant (%)[b]	13.0	11.0	8.9
Desires no more children (%)[a]	32.0	41.0	49.4
Mean ideal family size (number of children)[b]	6.2	5.8	4.4

[a]Among currently married women.
[b]Among all women.

SOURCES: Kenya (1980, 1986); Kenya National Council for Population and Development,
and Institute for Resource Development (1989).

modern method and also knew where to obtain such a method, and this level
of knowledge is true for both husbands and wives (data not shown). Some
90 percent of both husbands and wives approved of the use of family planning. This congruence of attitudes of husbands and wives extended also to
childbearing desires and intentions. Roughly half of both groups reported
that they wanted no more children. Ideal family size for both groups was
about 4.4 children, compared to 5.8 as recently as 1984. Thus, there is a
clear picture of widespread awareness and approval of family planning, and
of sharply increasing (and also more efficient) use of contraception.

We complete this overview of the main demographic trends in Kenya
with a brief look at the population distribution. Table 2-7 shows the number of urban centers (defined as having more than 2,000 inhabitants) in
Kenya for the four most recent census years, the growth rate of the urban
population, and the percentage of the population living in urban centers. In
general, the proportion living in urban areas is low, even in the most recent
census, but the rate of growth is considerably higher than the national rate
of growth, which suggests that considerable rural to urban migration has
been under way. Nairobi dominates the urban hierarchy and accounts for
some 40 percent of the total urban population (data not shown). Nairobi
has a drawing power that reaches throughout the country, although the majority of its migrants still appear to come from the Central and Eastern
provinces. Kisumu is the urban growth pole for the Western Province (the

TABLE 2-7   National Trends in Urbanization in Kenya Since 1962

Trend	1962	1969	1979	1989[a]
Total urban center[b] population (thousands)	748	1,080	2,309	3,705
Average annual rate of growth in population in urban centers between censuses	NA	5.4	7.6	4.7
Population living in urban centers (%)	9	10	15	17
Number of urban centers	34	47	92	124
Percentage of urban population living in Nairobi and Mombasa	70	70	51	49
Percentage of districts having urban population of				
<5%	NA	27	14	10
5-19%	NA	9	19	21
>20%	NA	5	8	10

NOTE: NA = not available.

[a]Provisional results from 1989 census.
[b]Defined as having more than 2,000 inhabitants.

SOURCE: Government of Kenya, Central Bureau of Statistics, data contributed for this report.

Lakes region) and Mombasa for the coast and northeast (see Shapiro, 1991, for more information on migration).[1]

SUMMARY

Kenya has experienced enormous economic and social changes in the 30 years since independence. Early economic success provided opportunities that have been taken. This bright beginning has become cloudy in the recent period. External shocks such as rising oil prices and falling prices of coffee have hurt the economy, and an apparent loss of domestic monetary and fiscal control has shaken donor confidence in the government's credibility. Even with past economic growth there is substantial poverty in Kenya, and social progress has brought rising expectations on the part of the Kenyan population. Distribution of income is almost certainly no less

---

[1]Migration remains the most underresearched area of Kenyan demography. Population movements of all types interact in important ways with fertility and mortality changes, and a full understanding of these latter trends can come only when there are better data to permit a deeper understanding of the migration streams in Kenya.

unequal than before, and for large segments of the population, per capita income has probably declined in the last 5 years. Because it will be many years before decreasing fertility brings a decline in new labor force entrants, employment creation will be a continuing problem in Kenya. The Kenyan economy is at an important turning point.

Demographically, Kenya seems well launched into its transition. Mortality has fallen and fertility now seems to be following, but overall growth remains rapid. Economic and social changes have led the way, with demographic changes following after a delay. Changes in the material conditions of life and also in the attitudes, aspirations, and motivations of the people seem to have been the driving forces behind the demographic changes. But government policies and programs have played a major role as well. Each of these factors is examined in later chapters.

3

Mortality Trends

CHILD MORTALITY

Child Mortality Before the Mid-1970s

Prior to the National Demographic Survey (NDS) of 1977 and the Kenya Fertility Survey (KFS) of 1977-1978, the only information on child mortality that covered all or most of the country came from the censuses. The first census in 1948 included questions on lifetime births to mothers, deaths at under 1 year of age, and deaths at over 1 year. These questions were asked in a purposive sample of communities. There was a broad age division of mothers between those within the reproductive ages and those past them. (Ages in calendar years were recorded for women who knew them, but the numbers were very small and unevenly distributed over the country.) From the responses, crude estimates of child mortality can be derived. At the censuses of 1962, 1969, and 1979, data were collected for all women in the reproductive period, by age, of total children born, surviving, and dead. The proportion dead by age group of mothers can be translated into approximate estimates of child mortality at different times by standard indirect methods.[1] The measures provide mortality trends over some 30 years from the 1940s.

---

[1] The procedure used here is the Brass child survival method (1964), which converts proportions of children ever born who have died, reported by women in five-year age groups, into estimates of the probability of dying (by age 5 in this report). In essence, the procedure uses

25

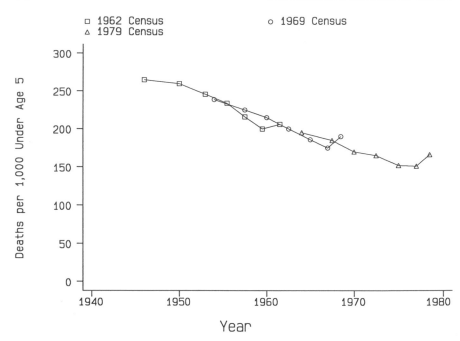

FIGURE 3-1   Trends in child mortality—indirect estimates of proportions dying.

These data have been thoroughly analyzed, particularly by John Blacker and colleagues (1987).   Results are available down to the district level, although they are not fully published.   Aggregate estimates of mortality up to age 5 years from the censuses (including a measure from the rather different 1948 source) are given in Figure 3-1.   They show a consistency among the different censuses that is remarkable relative to experience with the methods in other developing countries, particularly in Africa.   Thus the estimate for 1954 from the 1969 census (reports of women aged 45-49 years) is almost identical to the level at that time indicated by the 1962 census (women aged 30-34 and 35-39 years).   Similarly, the estimate for 1964 from 45- to 49-year-old women at the 1979 census is in excellent

---

an adjustment factor to translate the proportion dead into a life table value of mortality.   The adjustment factors are determined by the shape of the fertility schedule (United Nations, 1983).

   The resulting mortality estimates can be affected by sampling variation and reporting errors, such as the underreporting of children ever born, age misreporting, and the inclusion of still-births and adoptions in the number of children ever born.   In addition, there are a couple of important assumptions underlying this procedure: (1) that rates of change in infant and child mortality and fertility are constant in the recent period before the survey and conform to model schedules, and (2) that there is no association between a child's mortality risk and the mother's age or mortality.

TABLE 3-1 Indirect Estimates of Probability of Dying by Age 5 ($_5q_0$) per 1,000 Births from Census Reports of Children Who Have Died

Approximate Year of Estimate	$_5q_0$	Decrease per Year in Interval	Year of Census Data Source
1940	270	—	1948
1954	239	2.2	1969
1964	197	4.2	1979
1974	153	4.4	1979

agreement, with the points in the early 1960s derived from reports at the 1962 and 1969 censuses. Even the measure obtained from the 1948 census sample located around 1940 (not shown), which is less secure, is in accord with the extrapolation backward from later points. It can be concluded with confidence that the trend demonstrated by the series is valid, although reservations should be noted. There could be biases in the measures from errors common to censuses, for example, in the classification of stillbirths or the choice of model patterns of mortality by age in the estimation procedure. There are several alternative methods for arriving at estimates of the probability of dying by age 5 ($_5q_0$) and their time locations. However, the range of values from different assumptions is much smaller than the changes in incidence shown by the trend.

Child mortality fell from about 250 deaths per 1,000 births in 1950 to almost 150 by 1975, or at a rate of about 4 deaths per 1,000 births per year. Because the proportion of children dead for an age group of mothers is an average over a substantial range of child birth cohorts, the measures at calendar years are smoothed values around these points. The dips and upturns in the estimates from the reports for the younger mothers, apparent at all the censuses, can be attributed to selection by birth order and possibly social and economic factors such as illegitimacy. A fitted trend should smooth out these deviations. The trend is very nearly linear from 1950, and because this trend is based on a series of overlapping measures from three censuses there is no reason to believe it is an artifact of the method of estimation. Table 3-1 gives the estimates of $_5q_0$ at selected times based on the census data.

Child Mortality After the Mid-1970s

Between 1977 and 1984 there was a series of national surveys that collected information on children born and died by age of mother. Two of these, the 1977-1978 KFS and the 1984 Kenya Contraceptive Prevalence Survey (KCPS) were conducted with comparatively small samples (about

TABLE 3-2A Indirect Estimates of Probability of Dying by Age 5 ($_5q_0$) from Reports of Proportions of Children Who Have Died: Comparisons of Three Surveys and 1979 Census Data

Age of Mother	1978 KFS		1983 NDS		1984 KCPS		1979 Census	
	Year of Estimate	$_5q_0$	Year of Estimate	$_5q_0$	Year of Estimate	$_5q_0$	Year of Estimate	$_5q_0$
20-24	1975	.156	1980	.124	1981	.143	1976	.152
25-29	1973	.158	1978	.121	1979	.167	1974	.153
30-34	1970	.154	1976	.132	1977	.143	1972	.166
35-39	1968	.164	1973	.137	1975	.171	1970	.169
40-44	1965	.164	1971	.147	1972	.176	1967	.185
45-49	1962	.188	1967	.157	1968	.176	1964	.198

8,100 and 6,600 women interviewed, respectively) but obtained complete maternity histories. In the first survey, ages at death of children were also recorded and mortality rates in the time periods can be calculated directly. Three rounds of the NDS were completed in 1977, 1978, and 1983. There were problems with the analysis of the data from the first two dates, but some results are available for 1977. These are very similar to the measures estimated from the KFS but are rather erratic. They are not presented here. Table 3-2A gives estimates of $_5q_0$ derived from the proportions of children dead by age group of mothers, reported in three surveys, and compares them with the measures from the 1979 census. The values are also plotted in Figure 3-2.

The agreement among the four sets of indirect estimates is not as good as would be hoped. In assessing their characteristics it should be noted that the three surveys had essentially the same sampling frame, which excluded seven of the more remote districts of the country, as noted in Chapter 2. However, because only about 5 percent of the Kenyan population lived in these districts, the bias introduced in comparisons with the census results is very small. The sample errors of the estimates from the KFS and KCPS are considerable and may explain the erratic features of the individual measures of $_5q_0$. The census estimates are in best agreement overall with the KCPS

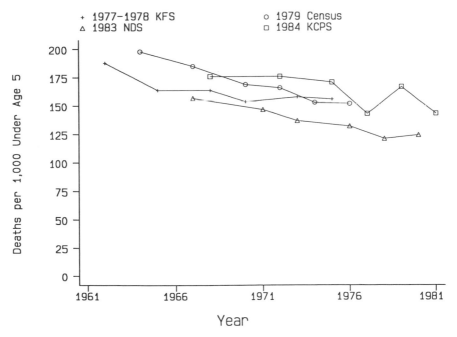

FIGURE 3-2 Trends in child mortality—indirect estimates of proportions dying.

child mortality levels, with both indicating quite a steep decrease in rates in the 10 years from the late 1960s. The measures derived from the reports of younger women in the KFS, providing child mortality levels around the mid-1970s, are also close to the census estimates. However, the KFS measures from reports of older women are considerably lower than the census values at equivalent times. The trend from the KFS is much flatter and fits rather poorly with the pattern of declines deduced from the 1962, 1969, and 1979 censuses. The outlying set of estimates is from the 1983 NDS, the general level being 20 to 30 deaths per 1,000 lower than the census rates, although the trend downward with time is steeper than for the KFS values.

Although there is some uncertainty about childhood mortality in the 1970s, a $_5q_0$ of about 155 deaths per 1,000 seems acceptable for around 1975. This estimate is in accord with the data from the 1979 census and the KFS. The proportions of children reported as dead by older women at the KFS may be a little understated, but the discrepancy here could be due to sample error. The level of child mortality shown by the NDS estimates is so inconsistent with the evidence from other sources that it must be rejected. There is no plausible explanation of why the NDS measures should be right, and the remaining series all show higher proportions of child mortality to much the same extent.

Of the surveys reviewed in Figure 3-2, only the KFS recorded dates of births and deaths of children. It is thus possible from these data to calculate the child mortality in calendar periods directly. (The estimates presented thus far have relied on indirect techniques and data that do not allow direct calendar period estimates.) Figure 3-3 compares the direct and indirect estimates from the KFS. The agreement is satisfactory. In accordance with the foregoing discussion, the KFS reports of child deaths in a recent period before the survey (here taken as 10 years) can serve as a reliable base for the examination of subsequent trends.

As discussed in Chapter 2, the Kenya Demographic and Health Survey (KDHS) of 1988-1989 collected maternity histories with details of births and deaths of children from 7,150 women aged 15-49 years. The sample frame was the same as for the KFS; the questions and procedures for obtaining information on child deaths were also very similar, but in the later survey there was a substantial additional section on child health. The comparability of data and coverage in the two surveys makes them the obvious sources for the measurement of child mortality changes over the 11-year interval.

Table 3-2B gives the indirect estimates of $_5q_0$ from data from the KFS and KDHS on proportions of children dead by age of mothers. The results are disquieting. The mortality rate in the mid-1970s of around 100 deaths per 1,000 births from the KDHS is only two-thirds of the rate from the KFS for the same period. The relative underreporting of child deaths in the

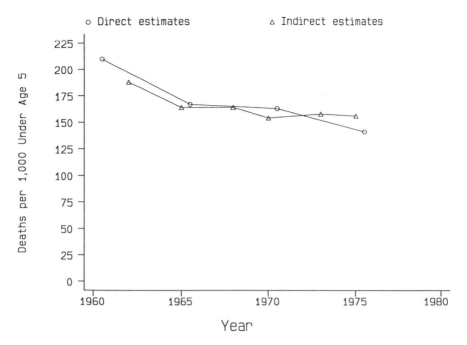

FIGURE 3-3   Estimates of $_5q_0$ (probability of dying by age 5) from 1978 KFS.

KDHS can be seen even more directly and obviously. At the KFS, 1.20 children per woman aged 35-39 years were reported to have died. Eleven years later at the KDHS, these women would have been 46-50 years old with additional deaths of children, including some of those born in the interval but failing to survive the heavy risks of infancy. However, only 1.08 dead children were recorded per woman aged 45-49 years.

It does not necessarily follow from the heavy relative underreporting of child deaths at the KDHS by the older women that there was a similar error for the younger women. The time trend in the $_5q_0$ derived from the age groups of mothers in the KDHS is effectively zero. The implication that there was no decline in child mortality over the 15 years or so before the date of the KDHS is, of course, completely at variance with the comparative levels of the two surveys and other evidence of regular improvements. Indeed, if a rate of decline in $_5q_0$ of 4 deaths per 1,000 per year is extrapolated from the experience of the 20 years before 1975 (based on census data), the resulting level of mortality by the mid-1980s is not very far from the KDHS estimates from the recent reports.

More incisive comparisons of the recording of child deaths at the KFS and KDHS are given in Tables 3-3A and 3-3B. Here the data from the later

TABLE 3-2B Indirect Estimates of Probability of Dying by Age 5 ($_5q_0$) from Reports of Proportions of Children Who Have Died, 1978-1989: KFS and KDHS Data

Age of Mother	1978 KFS			1989 KDHS		
	Year of Estimate	Children Dead per Woman	$_5q_0$	Year of Estimate	Children Dead per Woman	$_5q_0$
20-24	1975	0.23	.156	1986	0.14	.113
25-29	1973	0.54	.158	1984	0.28	.092
30-34	1970	0.85	.154	1982	0.52	.106
35-39	1968	1.20	.164	1979	0.67	.097
40-44	1965	1.45	.164	1977	0.84	.097
45-49	1962	1.88	.188	1973	1.08	.110

TABLE 3-3A   Child Deaths per Woman Reported from Births in Approximately the Same Periods—KDHS Estimates as a Percentage of KFS Estimates

Age of Women at KDHS	Years Before KDHS					
	10-14	15-19	20-24	25-29	30-34	More than 10
Under 35	91	99[a]				93
35-39	69	72	81[a]			72
40-44	72	73	69	65[a]		70
45-49	96	60	64	68	60[a]	67

[a]Including small numbers from earlier periods.

survey are backdated 10 years, and measures are calculated for 5-year age cohorts and preceding periods. This process is essentially a reconstruction of the KDHS results relevant to the years prior to 1979, slightly more than a year later than the KFS. Table 3-3A shows the ratios of child deaths reported per woman at the KDHS to those at the KFS for age cohorts of women in preceding time periods. Although the ratios are erratic in some of the marginal cells where the numbers of child deaths are low, the general pattern is coherent. The relative underreporting in the KDHS is about 30 percent for women aged 35 years and over, with only a slight tendency to become worse as age increases. At ages under 35 years, the discrepancy is much less, but because in this comparison only children of mothers under 25 years at the KFS are covered, the numbers of deaths are fairly small. A significant feature is the lack of any clear tendency for the ratios to be smaller for reports from the more distant past when the age group of the

TABLE 3-3B   Proportions of Children Reported Dead at KDHS and KFS from Births for Approximately the Same Time Periods and Cohorts of Mothers by Age Group

Age of Mothers at KDHS	KFS at Survey Date	10 Years Before KDHS	KDHS as a Percentage of KFS
25-29	.102	.087	85
30-34	.130	.107	82
35-39	.143	.103	72
40-44	.155	.115	74
45-49	.175	.127	73

mothers is fixed (comparing across the table). In Table 3-3B, the proportions of children dead as recorded at the two surveys for approximately the
same cohorts and time periods are displayed. The findings are in close
accord with the conclusions from Table 3-3A. The measures for the older
cohorts are about 27 percent lower from the KDHS than the KFS, with a
reduced shortfall for the younger cohorts. The discrepancies between the
reporting of child deaths in the two surveys decrease as the age of mother
decreases and also as births become more recent since the two characteristics are strongly correlated. It should be remembered, however, that the
comparisons are of deaths from births that occurred 10 more years before
the KDHS than the KFS.

Differentials in Child Mortality

Table 3-4 gives the comparisons of proportions of children reported
dead at the KFS and KDHS for approximately the same time periods and
cohorts by province, residence, and education. The cohorts distinguished
are the mothers under and over 35 years at the later survey. The numbers of
child deaths for the former category are frequently rather small for the
earlier date. Although the ratios of the measures at the two surveys are
fairly erratic, as expected in view of the sample errors, there is little indication of substantial variations in the relative completeness of reporting. Notably, the educational groups are in good agreement, with the smallest overall discrepancy in fact for the women with no education. The ratios for the
relative proportions of child deaths reported are higher for urban than for
rural women but only modestly; this suggests that reporting in urban areas
may be slightly better than in rural areas. For the provinces there are two
aberrant indices. In the Coast, the proportions of children reported as dead
by mothers under 35 years at the KDHS were much higher than at the KFS,
but the measures for mothers over 35 were in accord with the general pattern. The recorded proportions dead in Rift Valley for mothers over 35 at
the KDHS were exceptionally low. Although notable, these deviations do
not provide an adequate base for the derivation of incompleteness assess-
ments that differ for subgroups.

The reasons for the severe underreporting of child deaths at the KDHS
have not been established. One possibility is that the addition of more
detailed questions on birth intervals, contraception, and illness of children
overloaded the interviewers. There is no direct evidence that overloading
of the questionnaire affected the completeness of the reporting of deaths of
children who were born in the 10 years before the KDHS. The pattern of
error does not rule out the possibility that the reports for the recent period
were correct. There is, in fact, some evidence supporting this conclusion
from the distribution of child deaths over the 10 years before the surveys.

TABLE 3-4 Proportions of Children Reported Dead at KDHS and KFS from Births for Approximately the Same Time Periods and Cohorts of Mothers by Province, Residence, and Education

Residence and Education	Mothers Under Age 35			Mothers Age 35 and Over		
	KFS	KDHS	KDHS as Percentage of KFS	KFS	KDHS	KDHS as Percentage of KFS
Province						
Kenya	.125	.102	82	.158	.115	73
Nairobi	.083	.075	90	.129	.078	60
Central	.080	.045	56	.099	.080	81
Coast	.139	.265	191	.201	.168	84
Nyanza	.192	.142	74	.225	.179	80
Eastern	.091	.065	72	.142	.120	85
Rift Valley	.084	.063	75	.106	.046	43
Western	.143	.107	75	.194	.141	73
Residence						
Urban	.100	.085	85	.121	.098	81
Rural	.128	.104	81	.162	.116	72
Education						
None	.161	.135	84	.184	.140	76
1-4 years	.138	.126	91	.146	.097	66
5+ years	.092	.060	66	.109	.079	72

Calculations for the African Standard model life table (United Nations, 1982) give $_5q_0$ as 1.36 times the proportion of children dead from births in the preceding 5 years and 0.92 times the proportion for the 5 years before that (a ratio of 1.36/0.92, or 1.48). Thus, if child mortality is approximately constant, the proportion dead of births 5 to 10 years before should be about 50 percent greater than the proportion for 0 to 5 years. For the KFS the observed ratio of 1.60 is in good agreement with expectation, particularly if there is some decrease in mortality. For the KDHS the observed ratio at 1.17 seems much too low. Despite the crudeness of these calculations, they suggest that death reporting for recent births was much better than for the more distant events in the KDHS.

A measure of child mortality from the ratios of deaths to births in the 10 years preceding the surveys has been constructed as $0.68_5\delta_0 + 0.46_5\delta_5$ where $_5\delta_0$ and $_5\delta_5$ are the proportions of children dead from births in the preceding 5 years and the 5 years before that, respectively. The multiplying factors are derived from the relationships in the African Standard model life table with a simple averaging of the estimates from the two time periods. This measure is a satisfactory approximation for child mortality up to 5 years. It is, of course, possible from the maternity histories to calculate $_5q_0$ by more refined life table methods. Such calculations have indeed been made by Rutstein (1984) from the KFS data for provinces. The estimates from the approximate formula above are very close to the Rutstein values for the KFS, and the sample errors are considerable because of the small numbers of deaths. The simple procedure is adequate for the present purposes.

That there were substantial omissions of dead children in the KDHS reports has been established but the effect for births in the most recent 10 years is clearly much less than for more distant events. The trends and patterns by time suggest that an increase in the $_5q_0$ of 20 percent (a 17 percent omission of child deaths) would be a generous allowance for underreporting.[2]

Table 3-5 gives the estimates of $_5q_0$ by province, derived from survey reports of child deaths from births in the preceding 10 years, with and without adjustments for underreporting at the KDHS. Also given are the $_5q_0$ estimates for around 1954 obtained from the proportions of children dead at the 1969 census for women aged 45-49 years. As noted previously, these estimates lie on the trend line of national child mortality estimated from the

---

[2]The basis for the adjustment is the comparison of the KDHS and KFS birth histories (Table 3-3) and the trends from the age group estimates from the KDHS compared with the other censuses and surveys. This reasoning does not depend on the mortality levels in the periods preceding the KFS and the KDHS, which were used to estimate trends. In later discussions of the KDHS data, the 20 percent correction is applied to all subgroups.

TABLE 3-5 Estimates of Trends in Probability of Dying by Age 5 ($_5q_0$) by Province

Province	1954[a]	1973[b]	1984[c] Unadjusted	1984[c] Adjusted[d]	Ratios 1973/1954	Ratios 1984/1973 Unadjusted	Ratios 1984/1973 Adjusted[d]
Nairobi	.133	.103	.086	.103	77	84	100
Central	.192	.090	.049	.059	47	54	66
Coast	.223	.195	.151	.181	87	77	93
Nyanza	.328	.221	.153	.184	67	69	83
Eastern	.210	.130	.063	.076	62	48	58
Rift Valley	.167	.095	.051	.061	57	54	64
Western	.283	.191	.128	.154	67	67	81
Kenya	.239	.149	.091	.109	62	61	73

[a]From 1969 census.
[b]From births in 10 years before the KFS.
[c]From births in 10 years before the KDHS.
[d]Increased by 20 percent for omissions of deaths.

series of censuses. The ratios of the mortality levels in 1973 to 1954 and in 1984 to 1973 are also shown as summary indices of the trends. For Kenya as a whole, the decrease in $_5q_0$ is calculated to be 38 percent between 1954 and 1973, and 27 percent between 1973 and 1984, if the adjusted level is accepted. The assumption that no adjustment is needed gives a 39 percent decrease between 1973 and 1984. In either case, because the first interval is 19 years and the second 11, the rate of child mortality decrease accelerated in the late 1970s to 1980s.

The striking feature of the provincial breakdown is the high correlation between the reductions from 1973 to 1984 and from 1954 to 1973. The rankings of the decreases by size in the two periods for the provinces are very similar. It seems likely that the underlying determinants of improved child mortality in the recent period were the same as those operating over the previous 20 years or more. The provinces that appear as outliers from the average are Central, where an initial $_5q_0$ of 192 deaths per 1,000 becomes 59 deaths per 1,000 (adjusted), a reduction of 70 percent by the 1980s. At the other extreme, the Coast child mortality rate of 223 deaths per 1,000 in 1954 was below the national average; by the 1980s, it was two-thirds above the average at 181 per 1,000 (adjusted), a reduction of only 19 percent. Nairobi also appears to do rather badly in improvement from an exceptionally good level in 1954, but the changing composition of the city population must be borne in mind. The reductions in child mortality in the four remaining provinces were much closer to the national value of 54 percent, although it may be noted that the two with the higher initial levels (Nyanza and Western) did worse than the two that started from a more favorable base (Eastern and Rift Valley). As a result of these movements the variation in child mortality among provinces was relatively greater in the 1980s than in the 1950s, ranging from 59 to 184 per 1,000 (more than threefold) in the latter period compared with 167 to 328 per 1,000 (twofold) earlier if Nairobi is excluded.

The trends in $_5q_0$ between the 10 years preceding the KFS and the corresponding period before the KDHS are estimated in Table 3-6 by residence and education. The reduction appears to be slightly greater for rural areas, although if the indication that reporting of child deaths at the KDHS was a little better in urban communities was relied upon, the relative improvements would be virtually identical. The pattern of change by length of schooling does not suggest that education was a directly meaningful factor in the mortality declines. The differentials in the 1970s by residence and length of schooling were substantial and in the expected direction, but the further decreases in child mortality by the 1980s did not alter the relationships.

Measures of the levels of $_5q_0$ by education can be derived from the 1969 and 1979 census reports for the period 1954-1974 approximately, but

TABLE 3-6 Estimates of Trends in Probability of Dying by Age 5 ($_5q_0$) by Residence and Education

Residence and Education	1973[a]	1984[b]		Ratio 1984/1973	
		Unadjusted	Adjusted[c]	Adjusted	Unadjusted[c]
Residence					
Urban	.120	.090	.108	75	90
Rural	.152	.092	.110	61	72
Education					
None	.169	.106	.127	63	75
1-4 years	.139	.099	.119	71	86
5-8 years	.126	.087	.104	69	83
9+ years	.081	.062	.074	77	91

[a]From births in 10 years before the KFS.
[b]From births in 10 years before the KDHS.
[c]Increased by 20 percent for omissions of deaths.

the education categories are slightly different from those of the KFS and KDHS estimates, namely, none, primary, and secondary or above. The trends, however, are consistent with the 1973-1984 pattern of decline. They show a reduction from 244 deaths per 1,000 in 1954 to 184 per 1,000 in 1974 (75 percent) for children of mothers with no schooling; 160 to 121 (76 percent) for mothers with primary education; and a flat 67 deaths per 1,000 for the group with secondary schooling or higher. The low mortality of children of the well-educated mothers as long ago as 1954 reflects the highly selected composition of this very small class. However, by the time of the KDHS, about one-third of the women aged 20-24 years had been at school for 9 years or more. They represented a much wider cross-section of social and economic conditions. In 1954, the $_5q_0$ ranged from 244 per 1,000 to 67 per 1,000 for children of mothers with no schooling to those with secondary or above (nearly a fourfold ratio). The approximately corresponding estimates in 1984 (mothers with no education and those with 9 years or more) were 121 and 67 per 1,000, respectively (with a 20 percent upward adjustment to the KDHS reports of child deaths). The ratio at the later date was less than twofold. The reduction in variability and the very substantial improvement in the mortality of children for mothers with no schooling (a halving approximately between 1954 and 1984) show that factors other than formal education were powerful determinants of the changes over time, although in the cross-section, educational differentials remain.

The levels and trends in childhood mortality need to be examined at greater geographical disaggregation. Although some of the provinces in Kenya cover districts that are homogeneous in tribal composition, physical environment, and economic development, others are very diverse. Measures for districts have been calculated by Blacker and Airey[3] from the census reports by mothers of children born and died. Their results are not fully published but have been utilized in papers. Very similar results have been obtained by Ewbank et al. (1986). Unfortunately, it is not possible at present to extend these estimates to the late 1970s and 1980s. Calculations from the 1983 NDS have been made, but as shown previously the mortality levels are too low to be consistent with the other series. In any case the estimates would be brought forward only a few years. The combination of the underreporting of child deaths and the small sample sizes for districts in the 1989 KDHS makes the derived $_5q_0$ too unreliable for interpretation.

However, the strong correlation between the child mortality trends in the provinces from 1973 to 1984 and from 1954 to 1973 suggests that the district trends for the earlier years are broadly valid for the more recent period also. Of course there could still be individual exceptions. Evidence in appendix Table 3A-1 supports the general conclusion by demonstrating that the decreases in child mortality by district in Rift Valley Province in 1954 to 1964 were highly correlated with the declines in 1964 to 1974. It seems reasonable therefore to take the trends for 1954 to 1974 as good indicators of the variations in improvement by district over the past 30 years or so. Many of the districts show series of $_5q_0$ by period from the censuses that are in excellent agreement, as was the case for the national measures. In some cases the consistency is not so impressive. Examples in both categories are given in the appendix. In all, however, the calculations based on data from the 1969 and 1979 censuses provide a convincing trend.

Table 3-7 presents estimates of $_5q_0$ in 1954 and 1974 by district and the ratios of the latter values to the former. In all cases the 1974 measure is derived from the proportion of children reported as dead by mothers aged 25-29 years at the 1979 census. The corresponding child mortalities for provinces are not the same as the values for 1973 obtained from the KFS and utilized in Table 3-5, but the differences are remarkably small with the exception of Rift Valley Province where the 1979 census estimate is considerably higher than the KFS value (132 per 1,000 compared with 95 per 1,000). In this province, unlike the others, the proportion of dead children from births 5 to 10 years before the survey is exceptionally low, with an upward jump at 10 to 15 years. The value of 95 per 1,000 is likely to be an underestimate, but the gap to 132 is uncomfortably large. The estimates of $_5q_0$ in 1954 are derived from the reports of proportions of children dead by women aged 45-49 and 40-44 years at the 1969 census. In most districts the measure taken was that calculated from child deaths for the oldest group

---

[3]Thousands of calculations for population subgroups by different methods were made available to the working group from the files of Blacker and Airey.

TABLE 3-7 Estimates of Trends in Probability of Dying by Age 5 ($_5q_0$) by District

Province	District	1954	1974	Ratio 1974/1954
Nairobi	Nairobi	.133	.112	84
Central	Kiambu	.168	.077	46
	Kirinyaga	.255	.117	46
	Muranga	.214	.089	42
	Nyandarua	.188	.083	44
	Nyeri	.167	.062	37
Coast	Kilifi	.254	.236	93
	Kwale	.229	.224	98
	Lamu	.198	.198	100
	Mombasa	.168	.140	83
	Taita	.275	.142	52
	Tana River	.177	.189	107
Eastern	Embu	.217	.110	51
	Isiolo	.229	.153	67
	Kitui	.263	.177	67
	Machakos	.209	.119	57
	Marsabit	.152	.144	95
	Meru	.178	.103	58
Northeastern	Garissa	.176	.148	84
	Mandera	.141	.157	111
	Wajir	.207	.153	74
Nyanza	Kisii	.234	.133	57
	Kisumu	.337	.243	72
	Siaya	.355	.252	71
	South Nyanza	.370	.262	71
Rift Valley	Baringo	.206	.189	92
	Elgeyo Marakwet	.111	.150	135
	Kajiado	.146	.088	60
	Kericho	.156	.115	74
	Laikipia	.168	.098	58
	Nakuru	.190	.120	63
	Nandi	.187	.130	70
	Narok	.158	.120	76
	Samburu	.089	.098	110
	Trans Nzoia	.215	.138	64
	Turkana	.173	.158	91
	Uasin Gishu	.159	.114	72
	West Pokot	.253	.230	91
Western	Bungoma	.258	.170	66
	Busia	.362	.236	65
	Kakamega	.271	.168	62

of mothers (45 to 49 years). In a minority of districts, the series of $_5q_0$ values at time points derived from the 1979 and 1969 (and, in some instances, 1962) censuses indicated a trend line fitting poorly the estimate from the oldest group of mothers. In eight of these ten districts (as indicated in the table), the $_5q_0$ measure obtained from the reports of the 40- to 44-year-old mothers was selected as a better estimate for 1954, that is, more consistent with other points. In the other two districts, Marsabit and Laikipia, an average of the values from mothers aged 45-49 years and 40-44 years was taken. Although Marsabit is in Eastern Province, it is geographically in the remote north and was excluded from the KFS and KDHS samples. Three of the other districts with inconsistent reports of proportions of children dead by the oldest mothers in 1969 are in the Coast Province where improvement in child mortality was slight. The modified procedure of estimation makes the indices slightly more favorable but does not change the conclusion of poor gains. The other six districts are all in the diverse Rift Valley Province. Two of them, Baringo and Turkana, can be assessed in much the same way as the Coast Province districts above, but Narok, Laikipia, Trans Nzoia, and Uasin Gishu showed moderate improvements in child mortality and would still have done so, although to a different degree, if the estimation procedure had not been modified.

In the discussion of the levels and trends of $_5q_0$ by district, emphasis is placed on the cohesion or discrepancies with the provincial findings in Table 3-5. The outstanding gains in Central Province were shared by all of its districts fairly equally but with some advantage to Nyeri, both in level (62 per 1,000 in 1974) and in trend (a 63 percent improvement from 1954 to 1974). The three districts of Western Province were also notably similar in the $_5q_0$ trends, with reductions of about one-third from the high levels of 1954. The three districts in Eastern Province that adjoin Central (Embu, Machakos, and Meru) experienced falls in child mortality that were almost as great as for districts in Central and achieved respectably low levels in 1974. The areas of Isiolo and Kitui had average performances. As noted above, Marsabit is a geographically remote district compared with the rest of Eastern Province. Its child mortality appears to have improved little, although the 1974 level is not exceptionally high, when compared, for example, to most of Nyanza and Western provinces. The comments on Marsabit also apply to the three districts of Northeastern Province, which are also remote and were excluded from the KFS and KDHS samples. For these districts, there must be some suspicion about the accuracy of the estimates based on the reports of older women at the 1969 census and hence of the derived trends.

In 1954, Nyanza Province exhibited clearly the highest $_5q_0$, but by 1984 it had moved to a less extreme ranking. This change in ranking was due to average progress in three of the four districts (some 30 percent reduction from 1954 to 1974) and an impressive mortality decline of 43 percent in Kisii to a level of 133 deaths per 1,000, only about one-half of the measure in the rest of the province. Only one district in the Coast Province contradicted the trend as the province moved from average child mortality in 1954 to the highest incidence in 1974. This district was Taita-Taveta, the most distant from the Indian Ocean, where child mortality almost halved from 1954 to 1974 although from an initially high level. The 13 districts of the Rift Valley Province stretch from Kajiado, bordering Tanzania in the central-south to Turkana touching the Sudan in the remote northwest. Not surprisingly, the child mortality levels and trends are very diverse. The three districts that adjoin the Central Province (Nakuru, Laikipia, and Kajiado) experienced strong improvement to low levels, whereas the five in the northwest (Baringo, Elgeyo Marakwet, West Pokot, Samburu, and Turkana) made little gain. The remainder, lying between the central area and the west did comparatively well, although the mortality reductions were not as large as in Central Province and its immediately surrounding areas.

The Possible Effects of AIDS on Child Mortality

There has been increased concern about the spread of acquired immune deficiency syndrome (AIDS) in Kenya, as well as other regions of sub-Saharan Africa. One study of blood donors conducted in Nairobi indicated that the prevalence rate of human immunodeficiency virus (HIV), which causes AIDS, was 6.2 for men and 2.9 for women. In Nyanza and Coast provinces, the prevalence of HIV infection in blood donors was 4.3 and 3.5 percent, respectively. HIV seroprevalence rates for prostitutes in Nairobi have risen dramatically between 1980 and 1990, from 7.1 to 87.8 (Center for International Research, 1991).

There is little evidence on the effects of AIDS on child mortality in Kenya. There are certainly both direct and indirect effects. HIV is transmitted directly from infected mothers to their children during delivery (about 30 percent of the time), and possibly through breastfeeding. Children who are HIV negative, but whose mothers suffer from or die of AIDS face additional mortality risks from being orphaned (Working Group on the Effects of Child Survival and General Health Programs on Mortality, 1993). The mortality rates examined in this chapter are mainly for periods some time in the past when the effects of AIDS were very small. Recent child mortality rates most likely have been affected by AIDS, but the estimated addition to deaths is still probably small relative to the degree of measurement error. For Africa as a whole, the Working Group on the Effects of Child Survival and General Health Programs on Mortality (1993) estimates that AIDS is the primary cause of death in about 3 percent of all infant and child deaths.

ADULT MORTALITY

Information on adult mortality in sub-Saharan Africa is limited and uncertain. It is difficult to draw firm conclusions from the evidence for a single country such as Kenya. In particular, although broad trends in adult mortality for subnational aggregates can be explored, any findings are greatly restricted in time and must be hedged with cautions. A general review of the topic over a range of countries is given by Timæus (1993). The 1969 and 1979 censuses of Kenya included questions on the survivorship of parents. Both Ewbank et al. (1986) and Blacker et al. (1987), by similar techniques, used the responses to estimate the levels of adult mortality for Kenya as a whole as well as for its provinces and districts. A primary objective of the latter authors was to examine the relation between adult and childhood mortality. The account here is based on their estimates.

The method used was developed by Timæus (1986), following suggestions made by Preston and Bennett (1983). The proportion of persons in each age group with mothers (fathers) alive at the two censuses were averaged and adjusted to produce a single set of measures for females (males)

TABLE 3-8   Estimates of Adult Mortality, 1969-1979, Both Sexes

Province and District	Expectation of Life at Age 15, $e(15)$	Province and District	Expectation of Life at Age 15, $e(15)$
Kenya	52.9	Western	54.1
Nairobi	54.5	Bungoma	54.8
Central	55.7	Busia	50.7
Kirinyaga	57.1	Kakamega	54.9
Muranga	55.5	Northeastern	50.8
Kiambu	54.0	Garissa	49.9
Nyandarua	56.7	Mandera	50.6
Nyeri	56.3	Wajir	51.9
Eastern	54.4	Rift Valley	54.4
Embu	54.9	Baringo	50.5
Isiolo	50.5	Elgeyo Marakwet	52.4
Kitui	53.9	Kajiado	52.5
Machakos	55.5	Kericho	53.6
Marsabit	51.1	Laikipia	55.0
Meru	53.6	Nakuru	54.7
Coast	53.9	Nandi	54.7
Kilifi	54.0	Narok	56.6
Kwale	53.6	Samburu[a]	51.9
Lamu	52.2	Trans Nzoia	54.0
Mombasa	52.7	Turkana[a]	45.1
Taita Taveta[a]	50.7	Uasin Gishu	54.9
Tana River[a]	46.5	West Pokot	49.8

[a]Estimates based on 1979 orphanhood data only.

for the intercensal period. These proportions were then translated into probabilities of survival by the original weighting method devised by Brass and Hill (1973). The probabilities were finally converted into equivalent values of life expectancies at age 15, $e(15)$, by using the logit model life table system. The resulting $e(15)$ values were 55.2 and 50.5 years for females and males, respectively, for the country as a whole. The corresponding measures for 1979 derived by Ewbank et al. (1986) using slightly different methods were 55.2 and 51.4, in good agreement.

Table 3-8 presents the $e(15)$ values for provinces and districts. The measures for the two sexes have been combined. Although the variations in differentials by sex over the districts are by no means extraordinary, it is considered that little weight can be put on their precise values. The provincial indices of $e(15)$ are all close to the country-wide level. Although Central Province with the lowest child mortality has the highest life expectancy at age 15 (55.7 years), this level is only slightly greater than the measures for Western and Coast provinces, whose probabilities of child death by age 5 are more than double that of Central. The only province with an appreciably lower $e(15)$ is the remote Northeastern Province where, in any case, the estimates are of doubtful reliability. In Figure 3-4, the

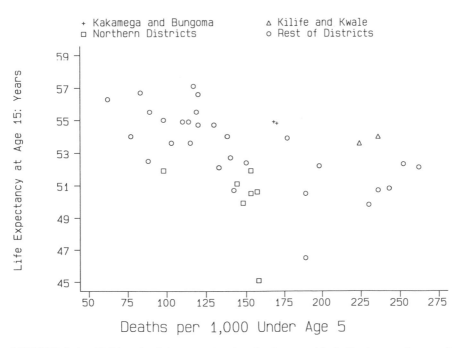

FIGURE 3-4   Child and adult mortality by district, specified districts, and rest of Kenya.

$e(15)$ measures are plotted against the $_5q_0$ estimates for 1974 by district. There is a general relationship of the kind expected but of very moderate strength. This result is perhaps not surprising in view of the comparatively small range of the $e(15)$s and their likely errors. The main divergences from a broadly linear relationship between adult and child mortality are for the remote districts of the north (indicated by squares). All seven of these, the areas not included in the KFS and KDHS samples, have adult life expectancies that are low relative to their $_5q_0$ estimates. It is possible that these inconsistencies are due to underreporting of child deaths, but it is equally plausible that nomadic ways of life lead to differences in the life table patterns. Some, but not all, of the districts in Coast and Western provinces present the reverse phenomenon, comparatively high adult life expectancies with heavy child mortality as in Kilifi and Kwale (shown as triangles), and Kakamega and Bungoma (pluses).

SUMMARY

From 1950 to 1975, child mortality in Kenya fell from about 250 to about 155 deaths per 1,000 births or at a rate of approximately 4 deaths per 1,000 each year. Analysis of the Kenya Demographic and Health Survey indicates substantial underreporting of child deaths, particularly by women aged 35 years and over, which makes the exact measurement of child mortality more difficult for the recent period. However, the evidence points to a more rapid decline from the mid-1970s to the mid-1980s to about 110 deaths per 1,000 (adjusted for underreporting) in 1984.

Mortality declines by province for the two periods, 1954-1973 and 1973-1984, were highly correlated, suggesting that the factors affecting decreased child mortality were similar for both periods. The pattern of declines between these two periods resulted in a greater variation among the provinces in child mortality in the 1980s than in the 1950s. The sizes of the reductions in mortality were similar for both urban and rural areas, although differentials in mortality by residence remain. Differentials in mortality by education were reduced, and remarkable gains were made in the mortality of children for mothers with no education.

APPENDIX

TABLE 3A-1   Estimates of Trends in the Probability of Dying by Age Five $(_5q_0)$ by District

Province and District	A 1954	B 1964	C 1974	Ratio B/A	C/B	C/A
Central						
Kirinyaga	.255	.184	.117	72	64	46
Muranga	.214	.148	.089	69	60	42
Kiambu	.168	.116	.077	69	66	46
Nyandarua	.188	.135	.083	72	61	44
Nyeri	.167	.111	.062	66	56	37
Coast						
Kilifi	.254	.250	.236	98	94	93
Kwale	.229	.232	.224	101	97	98
Lamu[a]	.198	.198	.198	100	100	100
Mombasa[a]	.168	.154	.140	92	91	83
Taita	.275	.206	.142	75	69	52
Tana River[a]	.177	.219	.189	124	86	107
Eastern						
Embu	.217	.162	.110	75	68	51
Isiolo	.229	.189	.153	83	81	67
Kitui	.263	.219	.177	83	81	67
Machakos	.209	.157	.119	75	76	57
Marsabit[b]	.152	.150	.144	99	96	95
Meru	.178	.148	.103	83	70	58
Northeastern						
Garissa	.176	.160	.148	91	92	84
Mandera	.141	.167	.157	118	94	111
Wajir	.207	.164	.153	79	93	74
Rift Valley						
Baringo[a]	.206	.209	.189	101	90	92
Elgeyo	.111	.156	.150	141	96	135
Kajiado	.146	.103	.088	71	85	60
Kericho	.156	.132	.115	85	87	74
Laikipia[b]	.168	.141	.098	84	70	58
Nakuru	.190	.158	.120	83	76	63
Nandi	.187	.163	.130	87	80	70
Narok[a]	.158	.139	.120	88	86	76
Samburu	.089	.109	.098	122	90	110
Trans Nzoia[a]	.215	.176	.138	82	78	64
Turkana[a]	.173	.173	.158	100	91	91
Uasin Gishu[a]	.159	.147	.114	92	78	72
West Pokot	.253	.263	.230	104	87	91

[a]1954 measure is estimated from the proportion of children dead for women aged 40-44 years.

[b]1954 measure is average of estimates for women aged 40-44 and 45-49 years.

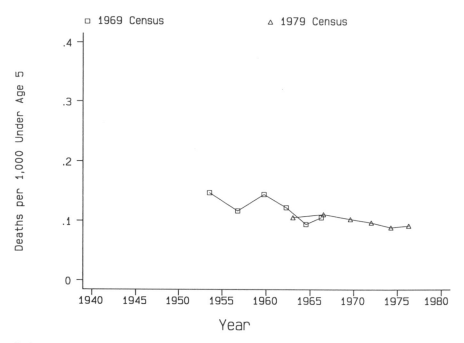

FIGURE 3A-1   Child mortality estimates—Kajiado district.

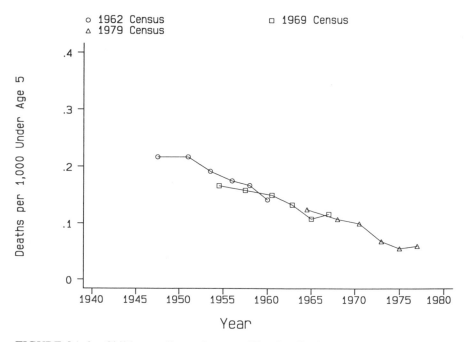

FIGURE 3A-2   Child mortality estimates—Kiambu district.

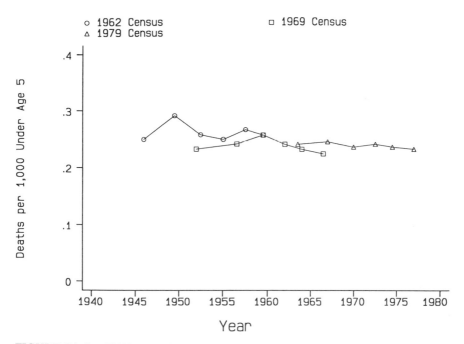

FIGURE 3A-3   Child mortality estimates—Kwale district.

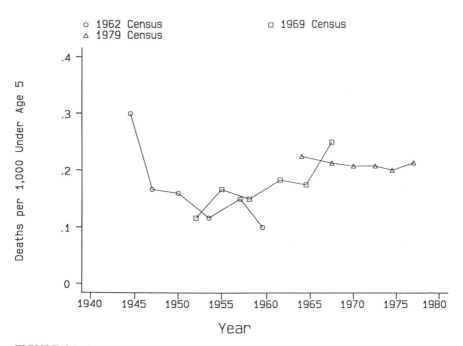

FIGURE 3A-4   Child mortality estimates—Tana River district.

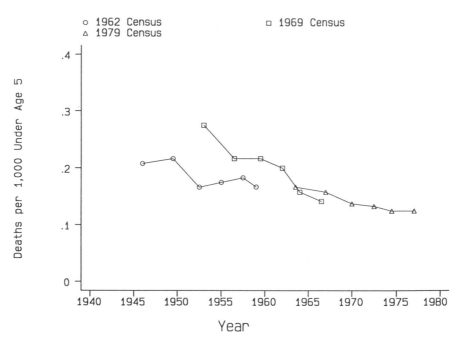

FIGURE 3A-5   Child mortality estimates—Trans Nzoia district.

4

Fertility Trends

Although reports of births in recent periods preceding the census and surveys were collected, they are subject to biases of coverage and time location errors. Adjustments can be made but not with any certainty. It is simpler to examine the trends in fertility through the ratios of children ever born to women in age groups. These measures are shown in Table 4-1 for the three censuses (1962, 1969, 1979), the Kenya Fertility Survey (KFS), the Kenya Contraceptive Prevalence Survey (KCPS), and the Kenya Demographic and Health Survey (KDHS). Values are given separately for the first and third rounds of the National Demographic Survey (NDS) (1977 and 1983); the data from the second round have not been closely analyzed. Panel A of the table gives the mean parities, that is, the total children born divided by the total women in the age group; panel B shows the percentage of women in each age group reporting no children; panel C presents mean births to mothers (instead of all women). On a first inspection of panel A, the pattern of change over time is clear enough. The mean parities of the younger women show little change up to 1984. The levels for the older women increase steadily until the late 1970s. However, the large-scale operations—the NDS and the 1979 census—give lower mean parities for women over 40 years of age in comparison with the KFS and KCPS, which were close to them in time. These differences suggest that there was underreporting of births at the census and the NDS of 1983. It seems likely that there was at least as much underreporting at the earlier censuses, and this conclusion is supported by the configuration. The mean parity of 5.07 for women aged 35-39 in 1962 rises by about 1.5 children for the same

TABLE 4-1 Birth Measures from Censuses and Surveys

Age Group of Women	1962 Census	1969 Census	1977 NDS	1978 KFS	1979 Census	1983 NDS	1984 KCPS	1989 KDHS
A. Mean Parities per Woman								
15-19	0.36	0.35	0.33	0.35	0.32	0.29	0.35	0.28
20-24	1.65	1.88	1.83	1.84	1.85	1.75	1.96	1.58
25-29	3.01	3.65	3.72	3.76	3.65	3.56	3.96	3.47
30-34	4.20	5.11	5.55	5.55	5.38	5.36	5.70	5.01
35-39	5.07	6.00	6.67	6.82	6.47	6.66	7.04	6.48
40-44	5.61	6.44	7.25	7.59	7.02	7.43	7.84	7.36
45-49	5.90	6.69	7.46	7.88	7.17	7.65	8.15	7.63
B. Percentage of Childless Women								
15-19	79.1	75.5	77.3	73.9	78.4	77.8	73.2	78.6
20-24	36.8	24.7	24.2	19.1	26.6	22.9	19.7	21.5
25-29	22.3	11.1	7.6	5.4	10.9	7.3	4.9	5.3
30-34	17.8	8.2	4.6	3.3	7.9	3.9	4.2	2.9
35-39	15.3	7.6	5.1	1.6	7.0	3.6	2.6	2.2
40-44	14.4	7.8	4.1	3.4	7.5	2.9	3.1	2.3
45-49	13.7	8.0	4.6	2.8	7.6	2.8	3.3	2.8
C. Mean Births per Mother								
15-19	1.71	1.45	1.45	1.34	1.48	1.32	1.31	1.31
20-24	2.61	2.50	2.41	2.27	2.52	2.27	2.44	2.01
25-29	3.87	4.11	4.02	3.98	4.10	3.84	4.16	3.66
30-34	5.11	5.56	5.82	5.74	5.85	5.58	5.95	5.16
35-39	5.99	6.50	7.03	6.93	6.96	6.90	7.23	6.63
40-44	6.55	6.99	7.56	7.86	7.59	7.65	8.09	7.53
45-49	6.84	7.26	7.82	8.11	7.76	7.87	8.43	7.85

cohort by 1969, too large an increase to be accounted for by additional births at these late ages. Part of the discrepancy can be attributed to the inclusion of women who did not report numbers of children with childless women at the censuses and NDS. The lower percentages of childless women in the 1977 and 1978 surveys at ages beyond which first births rarely occur (panel B), compared with the measures in 1969 for the same cohorts, must be due to error. This source of bias is eliminated in panel C in the measures of mean births per mother because women who did not report children are not included in the measure. However, the trends remain similar to those of panel A, although they are reduced in magnitude. There remains uncertainty about whether the apparent increase in fertility in the 1960s and 1970s was real or due entirely to improved birth reporting. On balance, the evidence suggests that there was an increase in fertility. The relatively lower estimates from the 1948 census analysis were supported by some small surveys, and the mean births per mother by age group in 1962, 1969, and 1979 are consistent with a gradual rise in fertility for cohorts born in the 1930s. A similar conclusion was reached from the detailed analysis of the KFS birth histories (Henin et al., 1982).

More recent attempts to examine fertility trends in Kenya use the parity progression ratio (PPR; the proportion of women going from an *n*th to an (*n* + 1)st birth). This index is a sensitive measure of fertility change but is very robust to data errors, for example, in time location of births and confusion between childlessness and failure to report. These ratios can be calculated directly for women past the ages of childbearing. In practice, the end of childbearing can be taken as 40 years because births after that age have a negligible effect on the PPRs except at very high birth orders. From the Kenya censuses, PPRs for age groups of women were calculated by Feeney (1988), up to 70-74 years of age for 1962 and 1979, and up to 60-64 years for 1969. He plotted the PPRs of each order on a time scale of year of birth of the woman so that the measures for the same cohorts at the three censuses were at coincident points on the horizontal axis. Blacker, in an unpublished note, extended Feeney's work by adding PPRs from 1969 and 1979 reports of births to women still in the childbearing period. The extrapolation to the end of reproduction was based on the fertility rates by birth order calculated from the births reported for the 12 months before the censuses. The method was developed by Brass (1985). Blacker also added measures from older women (more than 46 years of age) at the 1948 census and from those aged 45-49 years at the KFS and the KCPS. His graphs are reproduced in Figure 4-1.

The picture that emerges from the investigation of these measures is a coherent one. The comparable PPRs are higher for each successive census but only slightly for 1979 versus 1969. The 1962 values vary rather erratically over time, but the 1969 and 1979 trends are more regular. At every

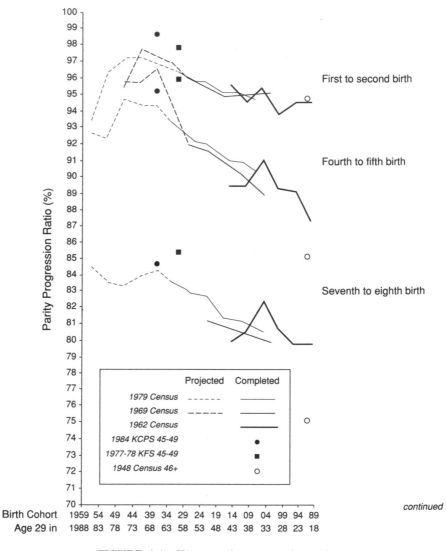

continued

FIGURE 4-1   Kenya parity progression ratios.

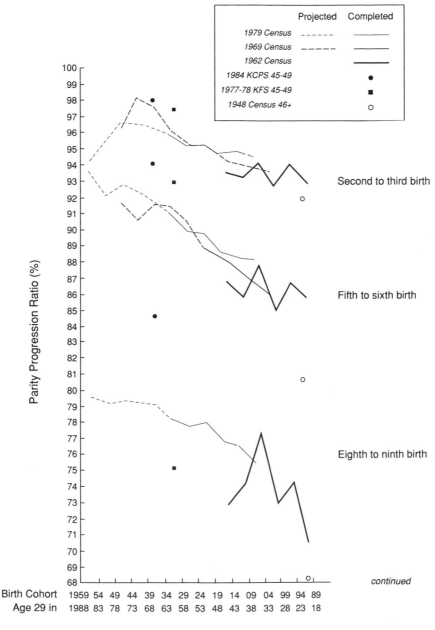

continued

FIGURE 4-1 *Continued*

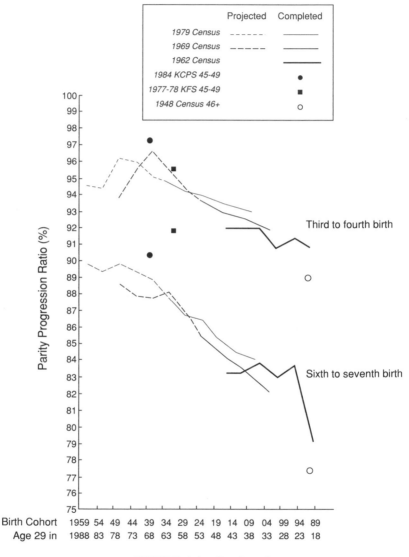

FIGURE 4-1 *Continued*

birth order there is a steady decline in the PPRs that extends from the 1970s back as far as the records go, that is, to women born around the beginning of the century. The pattern of the PPRs confirms that there was improved reporting in the censuses. It is possible that better reporting by younger women than by older contributed to the apparent rise in the PPRs over time. On the other hand, the closeness of the 1969 measures to the 1979 values for the same cohorts reported when 10 years older makes this possibility implausible. The extra PPRs derived by Blacker from the reports by younger women at the 1969 and 1979 censuses refer to more recent time periods. They suggest a cessation of the rise in the 1970s, and even possibly a decrease, but the synthetic nature of the calculations, projected by the use of current fertility reports, must signal caution. Blacker pointed out that the steepness of the rise in the PPRs between 1920 and 1970 increases with parity. This pattern casts doubts on the conclusion that the fertility increases were due mainly to decreases in pathological sterility. Blacker suggested that the main causes may have been biosocial factors, such as shorter birth intervals due to declines in breastfeeding and postpartum abstinence, along with lengthening reproductive lives. However, there are virtually no data on the proximate determinants of fertility prior to the late 1970s.

The surveys between 1977 and 1984 provide mean parities by age group of women that fluctuate but reveal no clear trend (Table 4-1, panel A). The sample errors, particularly for the older women, are appreciable, and the variations can be accounted for by chance and by small systematic biases in coverage and age reporting. The deduction is that the tendency for fertility to increase had ended. Of course, women at the end of their reproductive periods around 1980 had their peak childbearing in the 1960s. The substantial rise in fertility was probably a product of factors in the 1940s and 1950s, a finding that agrees with the analysis of the KFS birth histories (Henin et al., 1982) and an unpublished analysis in 1981 by the Panel on Tropical Africa of the Committee on Population and Demography.

In contrast to the surveys bracketing 1980, the 1989 KDHS gives mean parities that are distinctively lower. The striking reductions are for the younger age groups of women. Thus, the 2.01 and 3.66 mean births per mother at the KDHS for age groups 20-24 and 25-29 years, respectively (Table 4-1, panel C), are below all the other levels in the series from 1962 onward. The implication is that a sharp decline in fertility occurred in the 1980s. The 1983 round of the NDS is consistent with this conclusion, with slightly lower mean parities than the 1977 first round and the 1978 KFS for women age 20-34 years. The measures from the 1984 KCPS are contradictory, however, since they are the highest of the whole series. Nevertheless, the authors of the KCPS report discerned a slight decrease in current fertility from the KFS level on the basis of recent births. The evidence of fertility reduction from the KFS and KDHS comparison is examined in detail below.

EVIDENCE OF DECLINES IN FERTILITY
FROM RECENT SURVEYS

There have been many analyses of the KFS data. The main aim here is to establish a base for the study of subsequent fertility change in the 1980s. This brief exposition follows closely the approach in the report by Henin et al. (1982) published by the World Fertility Survey program. However, for the convenience of later comparisons, the birth measures are arranged by cohorts of women in time periods rather than in time periods by age groups of women. In the latter form, the age-specific rates are for the conventional five-year groups; in the former, for the intervals in which a cohort of women moves from one age group to the next (e.g., from 20-24 to 25-29 years). Table 4-2A shows the age-specific birth rates for cohorts of women, denoted by their ages at the time of the KFS, in five-year time intervals before the survey. The cumulated values of these rates from the beginning of childbearing up to five yearly time points are given in Table 4-2B. These represent what the mean parities would have been for the same women reporting in the same way at surveys 5 years, 10 years, and so on previously.

Summation of the rates within time periods gives the cumulated fertilities up to the highest age groups of women reporting; these are increasingly truncated as the past recedes. The measures for the preceding four time periods are shown in Table 4-2C. Comparison of the cumulated fertilities at equivalent ages along the top diagonal suggests that there had been a quite remarkable trend, with a sharp increase at 10-14 years before the survey followed by a substantial reduction thereafter.

Simple, approximate estimates of the fertility up to the 45-49 age group (very close to the total fertility) are obtained by assuming that the age-specific rates removed by the truncation are the same as for the women aged 45-49 years at the time of the survey. If, in fact, a decline had occurred, these extrapolations would lead to an under- rather than an over-estimation. The outcome is a total fertility of 9 births per woman in the 10-14 years before the survey, falling to 8.3 in the previous 5 years. The level indicated for 1963-1967 (10 to 14 years before KFS) is well above that deduced from census data near that time; the apparent trend is highly implausible and hard to explain in terms of changes in nuptiality, fertility control, or biological factors.

Examination of the age-specific birth rates in Tables 4-2A and 4-2B reveals that the distributions change over cohorts. The cumulated totals to equivalent ages rise over time for cohorts up to 30-34 years but decrease for

TABLE 4-2A Births per 1,000 Women by Age Groups and Time Period, KFS 1978

Age at KFS	Time Preceding Survey (years)								Total Births
	0-4	5-9	10-14	15-19	20-24	25-29	30-34	35+	
15-19	334	11							345
20-24	1,439	383	21						1,843
25-29	1,804	1,463	449	25					3,741
30-34	1,641	1,852	1,570	479	34				5,576
35-39	1,402	1,711	1,850	1,379	437	49			6,828
40-44	1,029	1,530	1,787	1,614	1,209	372	10		7,551
45-49	615	1,138	1,582	1,577	1,557	1,112	292	25	7,898
Total	8,264	8,088	7,259	5,074	3,237	1,533	302	25	

TABLE 4-2B Cumulated Births per 1,000 Women by Age Group, KFS 1978

Age at KFS	Time Preceding Survey (years)						
	0	5	10	15	20	25	30
15-19	345						
20-24	1,843	404					
25-29	3,741	1,937	474				
30-34	5,576	3,935	2,083	513			
35-39	6,828	5,426	3,715	1,865	486		
40-44	7,551	6,522	4,992	3,205	1,591	382	
45-49	7,898	7,283	6,145	4,563	2,986	1,429	317

TABLE 4-2C Cumulated Births per 1,000 Women by Time Period, KFS 1978

Age at KFS	Time Preceding Survey (years)			
	0-4[a]	5-9	10-14	15-19
30-34	5,218			
35-39	6,620	5,420		
40-44	7,649	6,950	5,677	
45-49	8,264	8,088	7,259	5,074
Extrapolated to 45-49	8,264	8,703	9,012	8,409
Adjusted	7,910	8,053	8,120	7,836

[a]Small undercount because no births recorded for women currently 10-14.

TABLE 4-2D Births per 1,000 Women by Age Group and Time Period: Observed and Model

Age at KFS	Source	Time Preceding Survey (years)				Total Births
		0-4	5-9	10-14	15-19	
30-34	Observed	1,641	1,852	1,570	479	5,576
	Model	1,693	1,823	1,551	499	
35-39	Observed	1,402	1,711	1,850	1,379	6,828
	Model	1,387	1,653	1,778	1,513	
40-44	Observed	1,029	1,530	1,787	1,614	7,551
	Model	946	1,342	1,598	1,721	
45-49	Observed	615	1,138	1,582	1,577	7,898
	Model	344	947	1,342	1,599	

older cohorts (when comparing along the diagonals in Table 4-2B). The variation is relatively slight up to the 35-39 age cohort, but sharp for the two oldest groups of women. Thus, for fertility up to age 30-34, 37 percent (2,083 divided by 5,576) was reported as before age 20-24 for the 30-34 age cohort, but only 31 percent (1,429 divided by 4,563) for the 45-49 age cohort. This difference might occur because of a move to earlier childbearing, but it seems unlikely and there is no evidence for it. A more convincing explanation (particularly since the same feature has occurred in several birth history surveys of populations with a low literacy level) is recording error in which the births are located too near the present time. Corrections are made by fitting the observations for cohorts aged 30-34 and 35-39 years by the relational Gompertz model (Brass, 1981). The two parameters of the model distribution are taken as rounded averages over the two cohorts. The observed age-specific rates for the two oldest cohorts are then replaced by the values from the model distribution, with their sums constrained to equal the observed cohort totals. As can be seen from Table 4-2D, the model values for the 30-34 and 35-39 cohorts are fairly close to the observed birth rates. Therefore, only the distributions for the two oldest cohorts have been adjusted. The total fertilities (to age 45-49 years), extrapolated from the adjusted measures in the same way as for the observed measures, are also given in Table 4-2C. The fluctuation in total fertility over the 20 years 1958-1977 has now largely disappeared, leaving a roughly constant level of about 8 children per woman for that period. Similar exercises allowing for systematic changes in the distribution of fertility by age of woman have been carried out. The estimates differ in detail, but the general conclusions are the same.

An alternative explanation of the time displacement of births in the reports of older women is age error. Perhaps, these women were on average younger than the recorded age span, and hence the cumulated fertilities were to earlier points of the reproductive period than specified. However, the bias would have to be very large, with women in the 45-49 years age group really about 3 years younger than reported relative to the 30-34 age group. Moving the average ages to bring the locations of the cohort time-period birth distributions into agreement would not bring them into near coincidence because those for the cohorts under age 40 have a more peaked shape than those for the older women. Nor, of course, would the time-period total fertilities be much changed, leaving the trend anomalies unexplained. Thus, the time-period shift seems to be much the most plausible explanation although there may easily be a contribution from systematic age biases.

Tables 4-3A, 4-3B, and 4-3C present the fertility measures from the KDHS maternity histories in the same form as Tables 4-2A to 4-2D for the KFS. Thus, the age-specific birth rates for cohorts and time periods are in

TABLE 4-3A Births per 1,000 Women by Age Group and Time Period, KDHS 1989

Age at KDHS	Time Preceding Survey (years)							Total Births
	0-4	5-9	10-14	15-19	20-24	25-29	30-34	35+	
15-19	272	9							281
20-24	1,269	300	11						1,580
25-29	1,558	1,415	470	29					3,472
30-34	1,359	1,665	1,445	498	48				5,015
35-39	1,190	1,550	1,780	1,477	448	29			6,474
40-44	728	1,360	1,663	1,647	1,433	501	30		7,362
45-49	326	1,011	1,488	1,526	1,672	1,256	326	20	7,625
Total	6,702	7,310	6,857	5,177	3,601	1,786	356	20	

TABLE 4-3B   Cumulated Births per 1,000 Women by Age Group,
KDHS 1989

Age at KDHS	Time Preceding Survey (years)						
	0	5	10	15	20	25	30
15-19	281						
20-24	1,580	311					
25-29	3,472	1,914	499				
30-34	5,015	3,656	1,991	346			
35-39	6,474	5,284	3,734	1,954	477		
40-44	7,362	6,634	5,274	3,611	1,964	531	
45-49	7,625	7,299	6,288	4,800	3,274	1,602	346

TABLE 4-3C   Cumulated Births per 1,000 Women by Time Period,
KDHS 1989

Age at KDHS	Time Preceding Survey (years)			
	0-4[a]	5-9	10-14	15-19
30-34	4,458			
35-39	5,648	4,939		
40-44	6,376	6,299	5,369	
45-49	6,702	7,310	6,857	5,177
Extrapolated	6,702	7,636	8,194	8,002
Adjusted	6,714	7,269	7,723	7,891

[a]Small undercount because no births recorded for women currently 10-14.

TABLE 4-3D   Births per 1,000 Women by Age Group and Time Period:
Observed and Model

Age at KDHS	Time Preceding Survey (years)					
	Source	0-4	5-9	10-14	15-19	Total Births
30-34	Observed	1,359	1,665	1,445	498	5,015
	Model	1,404	1,623	1,465	494	
35-39	Observed	1,190	1,550	1,780	1,477	6,474
	Model	1,190	1,501	1,709	1,544	
40-44	Observed	728	1,360	1,663	1,647	7,362
	Model	798	1,207	1,521	1,733	
45-49	Observed	326	1,011	1,488	1,526	7,625
	Model	268	797	1,206	1,521	

Table 4-3A; the cumulated fertilities from the start of childbearing for cohorts in Table 4-3B, and the summation over the rates in time periods in
Table 4-3C. As with the KFS sample, approximate estimates of fertilities
up to the age group 45-49 years in earlier periods are derived by substitut-
ing the age-specific rates removed by the truncation.

The signs of displacement in the time location of births are much less
evident in the KDHS than in the KFS maternity histories. The crudely
extrapolated total fertilities up to ages 45-49 in Table 4-3C give only a
slight indication of peaking 10-14 years before the survey, and the birth
distributions by age for cohorts are very similar up to the group 40-44 years
of age. Only for the 45-49 cohort does a configuration consistent with the
distortions for the KFS maternity histories occur. This distortion is illustrated by the calculation shown in Table 4-3D. As with the KFS data, the
observed birth rates over ages for the cohorts aged 30-34 and 35-39 years
were fitted by the relational Gompertz model. The averaged parameters
defined a distribution pattern that was taken to hold for the two oldest
cohorts also giving the model birth rates in Table 4-3D. The observed rates
were replaced by the model rates for the two oldest cohorts, and the total
fertilities to age 45-49 years were estimated by extrapolation. Because of
the apparent trends, the truncated upper tails of the birth histories were
completed from the model measures of the KFS. Thus the rates from the
KFS at 0-4 and 5-9 years before the survey were taken to represent the
missing upper value of the KDHS at 10-14 and 15-19 years earlier for the
appropriate cohorts. The small discrepancy due to the interval between the
surveys being slightly greater than 11 years rather than 10 is negligible at
the level of approximation.

The differences between the adjusted and crudely extrapolated total
fertilities are much smaller for the KDHS than for the KFS data, and indeed
it is possible that the adjustment has resulted in an overcorrection. The
assumption that the fertility pattern by age for cohorts had remained constant is much more plausible for the KFS maternity histories than for the
KDHS ones because of the near stability of rates in the former case. If, in
fact, the pattern for the two oldest cohorts at the KDHS is taken to be that
estimated from KFS observations, the resulting adjusted total fertilities to
ages 45-49 are close to the values extrapolated without adjustment. The
most direct method for the determination of fertility changes in Kenya is
comparing the birth rates for the period just before the KDHS with the
corresponding measures derived from the KFS. The examination in the
preceding paragraphs suggests that there will be little overall bias in such a
comparison. The fertility rates in the past 5 years seem to have been reported with little time location distortion in both surveys. There is more
uncertainty about the detailed trends over the 1970s and 1980s.

A direct assessment of the levels of reporting at the KDHS and KFS is

TABLE 4-4 Births per 1,000 Women Reported in KDHS and KFS for Approximately the Same Periods and Age Ranges of Women

	KFS	KDHS	KDHS Adjusted[a]
Age of Women at KDHS			
25-29	346	499	492
30-34	1,844	1,990	2,020
35-39	3,741	3,735	3,881
40-44	5,582	5,274	5,533
45-49	6,829	6,288	6,686
Time preceding KDHS in years			
10-14	6,623	6,845	6,973
15-19	5,422	5,178	5,448
20-24	3,892	3,601	3,881
25-29	1,885	1,786	1,915
30+	500	376	445

[a]Including estimates for omitted dead children.

obtained from births recorded at the two surveys for the same cohorts and time periods. If the intersurvey interval had been exactly 10 years, the organization of the check would have been very simple with the five-yearly grouping of ages and time. The actual interval of slightly more than 11 years requires awkward modification of tabulations or interpolation. Such calculations have been made, but the adjustments are so small compared with other factors (e.g., the sample error) that they can be ignored for the present purpose. In effect, the KDHS sample of women is back-dated 10 years, and the reporting of births up to then is compared with the KFS data as if there was a coincidence of time. The results are shown in Table 4-4.

In the first part of the table, the lifetime births up to the same ages are shown for the cohorts of women. The second part presents the reported births in given time periods. Chapter 3 shows that there was a substantial omission of dead children in the KDHS relative to the KFS. Measures with approximate adjustments for this omission are also presented in the table.[1] Agreement in the reporting of births in the two sources is remarkably close, particularly after the correction for omitted dead children. Of course, identical levels in the individual cells are not to be expected in the presence of sample variation, and of age and time location errors. There is no indication, however, that the completeness of reporting of surviving children dif-

---

[1]Adjustments for omitted dead children are not presented elsewhere in this chapter because their inclusion does not significantly alter the analyses. Adjustments are presented in Table 4-4 because the effect on comparisons of more distant KDHS reports with recent KFS ones is appreciable.

fered materially in the two surveys. It should be noted, in particular, that the births per 1,000 women 10-14 years before the KDHS (and 0-4 years before the KFS) are a little higher for the former. This difference may be a residual time location distortion of the typical form. There is no indication either that the KFS births in the 5 years before the survey have been appreciably overstated, or that there is consequently a significant bias in their use as a base for measuring fertility change.

Checks of the kind made in Table 4-4 can be applied for subgroups of the population, but conclusions can be only tentative because of the smaller numbers and larger sample variability. Comparisons for provinces, residence, and educational levels are shown in Tables 4-5A, 4-5B, and 4-5C.

TABLE 4-5A   Births per Woman Reported in KDHS and KFS by Age Group and Province in Approximately the Same Time Periods

Age of Women at KDHS	KFS	KDHS[a]	KFS	KDHS[a]
	Kenya		Nairobi	
25-29	0.35	0.45	0.39	0.35
30-34	1.84	2.02	1.31	1.54
35-39	3.74	3.88	3.43	3.12
40-44	5.58	5.53	4.98	4.23
45-49	6.83	6.69	6.96	5.46
	Central		Coast	
25-29	0.19	0.36	0.51	0.41
30-34	1.62	1.99	1.98	1.77
35-39	3.75	3.76	3.58	3.85
40-44	5.58	5.56	5.21	5.70
45-49	6.84	6.27	6.22	6.06
	Nyanza		Rift Valley	
25-29	0.40	0.57	0.44	0.64
30-34	2.01	2.35	1.94	2.09
35-39	3.78	4.19	3.81	3.95
40-44	5.58	5.65	5.75	5.82
45-49	7.21	7.67	6.78	5.70
	Western		Eastern	
25-29	0.34	0.44	0.24	0.42
30-34	2.15	2.16	1.67	1.66
35-39	3.97	3.96	3.61	3.59
40-44	5.95	5.69	5.48	5.07
45-49	7.11	7.55	6.62	6.41

[a]Adjusted.

TABLE 4-5B Births per Woman Reported in KDHS and KFS by Age Group and Residence in Approximately the Same Time Periods

Age of Women at KDHS	KFS	KDHS[a]	KFS	KDHS[a]
	Urban		Rural	
25-29	0.41	0.33	0.34	0.53
30-34	1.57	1.55	1.91	2.12
35-39	3.41	3.26	3.80	3.97
40-44	4.77	4.04	5.67	5.78
45-49	6.25	5.24	6.88	6.82

[a]Adjusted.

TABLE 4-5C Births per Woman Reported in KDHS and KFS by Age Group and Education in Approximately the Same Time Periods

Age of Women at KDHS	KFS	KDHS[a]	KFS	KDHS[a]
	No Schooling		1-4 Years	
25-29	0.75	0.80	0.32	0.75
30-34	2.07	2.25	2.09	2.37
35-39	3.71	4.03	3.94	4.07
40-44	5.54	5.46	6.03	5.82
45-49	6.57	6.53	7.50	7.47
	5-8 Years		9+ Years	
25-29	0.27	0.43	0.19	0.21
30-34	1.94	2.05	1.06	1.10
35-39	3.92	3.90	2.89	2.75
40-44	5.27	5.77	4.78[b]	3.32[b]
45-49	6.99	6.40	[c]	[c]

[a]Adjusted.
[b]32 and 30 women for KFS and KDHS, respectively.
[c]10 women or less.

For nearly all the subgroups there is no consistent tendency for the fertility reported over the same period to be significantly higher or lower from the KDHS or the KFS. The exceptions are Nairobi Province and urban residence (nearly half from Nairobi), where the KDHS births per woman are substantially lower than the KFS for the cohorts aged 40-44 and 45-49 years at the former survey. It is difficult to interpret these differences with confidence because of the large migration to and from Nairobi and the heterogeneous nature of the population. It would not be surprising if reporting by the Nairobi women of births that had occurred some time before, often in a different location, suffered from omissions. It does not necessarily follow that the reporting of recent births was similarly biased.

There is, of course, no external check on the accuracy of the number of births in the two 5-year intervals preceding the KDHS, but the generally good agreement overall and in most of the subgroups for the more distant periods inspires confidence. It is concluded that the total fertility was close to 8.2 births per woman in 1973-1977 and 6.7 in 1984-1988. The evidence is convincing that there was little, if any, fertility reduction before the mid-1970s but an appreciable decline in the later 1970s and the 1980s. The detailed trend cannot be determined with certainty, but the time schedule of births from the KDHS seems reliable. If this is accepted, the rate of decrease accelerated in the later 1980s.

DIFFERENTIALS IN THE DECLINES IN FERTILITY

The pattern of the decline at different stages of reproduction for Kenya and subgroups of the population is analyzed in Tables 4-6A, 4-6B, and 4-6C. The reductions in births per woman in the 5 years before the KDHS from the corresponding measures for the 5 years before the KFS are shown for three age ranges. Early reproduction refers to births to women at ages up to 20-24 years or up to approximately 22.5 years because the births were over the preceding 5 years; the middle stage refers to 25-29 and 30-34 years (fertility at approximately 22.5 to 32.5 years); later reproduction refers to ages over 35 (fertility after approximately 32.5 years). The purpose of grouping by stages is to reduce sample variability but to preserve biosocial differentiation. The measures calculated are of the reductions in births overall and for each reproduction stage, and the percentage contribution of each stage to the overall decline.

For Kenya as a whole, all age groups contributed to the overall fertility decline of 19 percent, but the reduction at the late stage was more than double those at earlier ages. Because more births occur at the middle stage, however, it contributed slightly more than the late stage to the total decline. The subpopulations (province, urban/rural, education) show appreciable variations in the fertility decreases and their composition by ages of women. Because

TABLE 4-6A Reduction in Total Fertility at Different Stages of Reproduction 1973-1977 to 1984-1988, by Province

Stage of Reproduction[a]	Fertility 1973-1977	Reduction	% Fall	% of Total
Kenya				
E	1.77	.23	13	15
M	4.85	.74	15	47
L	1.64	.59	36	38
T	8.26	1.56	19	100
Central				
E	1.58	.20	13	7
M	5.19	1.55	30	57
L	1.93	.95	49	35
T	8.70	2.70	31	100
Nyanza				
E	1.86	.04	2	4
M	4.75	.50	11	47
L	1.50	.53	35	50
T	8.11	1.07	13	100
Western				
E	2.02	.34	12	—
M	4.92	-.35	-7	—
L	1.50	.43	29	—
T	8.44	.42	5	—

Stage of Reproduction[a]	Fertility 1973-1977	Reduction	% Fall	% of Total
Nairobi				
E	1.43	.11	8	7
M	4.26	1.57	37	98
L	.46	-.07	-15	-4
T	6.15	1.61	26	100
Coast				
E	1.92	.71	37	35
M	4.14	.85	21	42
L	1.31	.45	34	22
T	7.38	2.02	27	100
Rift Valley				
E	2.00	.37	19	21
M	5.07	.91	18	53
L	1.73	.44	25	25
T	8.80	1.73	20	100
Eastern				
E	1.54	.13	8	10
M	4.87	.49	10	36
L	1.86	.74	40	54
T	8.27	1.36	16	100

[a]E = early, up to 20-24 years; M = middle, 25-29 to 35-39 years; L = late, 40-44 years and over; T = total.

TABLE 4-6B Reduction in Total Fertility at Different Stages of Reproduction, 1973-1977 to 1984-1988, by Residence

Stage of Reproduction[a]	Urban				Rural			
	Fertility 1973-1977	Reduction	% Fall	% of Total	Fertility 1973-1977	Reduction	% Fall	% of Total
E	1.59	0.28	18	19	1.82	0.21	12	15
M	3.83	0.83	22	58	4.96	0.63	13	44
L	0.75	0.33	44	33	1.70	0.59	35	41
T	6.17	1.44	23	100	8.48	1.43	17	100

[a]E = early, up to 20-24 years; M = middle, 25-29 to 35-39 years; L = late, 40-44 years and over; T = total.

TABLE 4-6C Reduction in Total Fertility at Different Stages of Reproduction, 1973-1977 to 1984-1988, by Education

Stage of Reproduction[a]	Fertility 1973-1977	Reduction	% Fall	% of Total
No Schooling				
E	2.18	0.18	8	16
M	4.62	0.40	9	35
L	1.63	0.57	35	50
T	8.43	1.15	14	100
5+ Years				
E	1.59	0.14	9	11
M	4.87	1.01	21	77
L	1.22	0.17	14	13
T	7.68	1.32	17	100

Stage of Reproduction[a]	Fertility 1973-1977	Reduction	% Fall	% of Total
1-4 Years				
E	1.96	-0.27	-14	-21
M	5.18	0.78	15	60
L	1.86	0.81	44	62
T	9.00	1.31	15	100

[a]E = early, up to 20-24 years; M = middle, 25-29 to 35-39 years; L = late, 40-44 years and over; T = total.

some of the sample sizes are quite small and there are signs of distortion from age and other misstatements, a part of the variability must be discounted as due to error. In the interpretation, only the most notable deviations can be confidently accepted as valid. Perhaps the major finding is the near universality of the fertility reductions in subgroups. With the exception of Western Province (see below), there were moderate to substantial declines in every category. The rural decline was only marginally smaller than the urban (17 versus 23 percent), with quite similar changes in the corresponding reproductive stages. Among the provinces, Central stands out for the high overall reduction (31 percent) with only a small contribution from the youngest women. The fertility decline in the Coast (27 percent) was also great, but was attained by a particularly large effect in the early reproductive stage, the drop at later ages being about average. The pattern for Nairobi is anomalous, with virtually no change at early or late ages but a heavy (37 percent) reduction in the middle reproductive stage. However, the Nairobi sample sizes were comparatively small, and as noted above, there are doubts about the stability of the estimates from the KFS to KDHS. The oddest results are for Western Province, where average fertility reductions at early and late ages were offset by a rise for the middle stage of reproduction to give an overall inconsequential decrease of 5 percent. It is difficult to find a sensible explanation for such a pattern of change. Alteration in forms of age error is possible but not plausible. The suggestion that the rise in the middle reproductive stage is an artifact due to improvement in reporting cannot be dismissed. If this were so, the true fall in fertility would be closer to the average for Kenya.

The striking feature of the results by level of education is the near equality of the fertility declines in the three categories: no schooling (14 percent), 1-4 years of schooling (15 percent), and 5 years or more of school (17 percent), despite appreciably different initial fertility levels. There was a rapid increase in the educational attainment of women in the interval between the two surveys, and the movement into higher groups leads to the larger reduction (19 percent) for Kenya than for any of the component groups. Changes in the composition of the education categories by other socioeconomic characteristics may have modified the size of the reductions but not by much. The women with no schooling at the time of the KDHS were a residual group considerably smaller in number than at the time of the KFS, particularly at the younger ages. In that context, the fertility reduction of 14 percent is even more notable.

PATTERNS OF FERTILITY DECLINE

Fertility decline comes mainly through two mechanisms: (1) reduction in the proportion of women at risk through changes in the pattern of mating (e.g., later age at marriage), and (2) decreased propensity for additions to families because of alterations in the factors of reproduction, most commonly, the use of contraceptive measures. The extent to which the decreases in Kenya occurred in the middle and late reproductive stages suggests that the second mechanism was dominant. It is difficult in African societies to isolate the effects of mating changes because of the complexity of behavior (see van de Walle, 1993), but a direct guide to family limitation can be obtained from the study of parity progression ratios, that is, the proportion of women in an age cohort who, having attained an nth birth, go on to higher orders. For cohorts who have completed their fertility, the calculations are direct and elementary. When the data available are birth histories of women still capable of bearing further children, as from the KDHS, the analysis technique is more complicated. For each birth progression, a life table form of calculation is required that allows for the removal of women from risk during the reproductive period. For each age group of women, the rates of movement from the nth to the $(n + 1)$st birth are computed by intervals (normally monthly) from the earlier birth. As the gap lengthens, the number of women whose experience extends that far is reduced, ultimately becoming too few for the calculations to be effective. However, most births occur within 5 years of the previous one. Accordingly, instead of the PPR (which can never be measured when fertility is incomplete) we investigate B_{60} (the proportion of women moving on to the next birth within 5 years). Estimates of B_{60}s can be made up satisfactorily to high birth orders for women over 30, and low to medium orders for the 25-29 and 20-24 cohorts. The specific definitions of high and medium depend on sample sizes, as well as levels and age patterns of fertility. However, the estimates of B_{60} are biased, slightly but significantly, by the truncation of birth histories. The women who will ultimately go to the $(n + 1)$st birth, but at a slower pace than average, will tend to be excluded from the calculation to a greater extent than those who bear children more rapidly, and the estimated B_{60}s are too high (Hobcraft and Rodriguez, 1980). The bias increases with the truncation and thus distorts the trend over cohorts. A simple but effective adjustment has been devised (Brass and Juarez, 1983; Juarez, 1983). The procedure is to compare the B_{60}s for adjacent cohorts with the preceding 5 years of births omitted for the older. Thus the B_{60}s for the group 20-24 years are set against the corresponding measures for the 25-29 cohort when these women were 20-24 years old. The ratios of the B_{60}s for the comparably truncated birth histories give the unbiased trends. It is assumed that the ratios of the equally biased B_{60}s are the same as those for the true B_{60}s, but over most of the range the adjustments are small. There is most doubt for the marginal estimates, that is, the highest birth orders for each cohort where the sample errors are also the largest.

Appendix Table 4A-1 shows the calculation of the basic B_{60}s for Kenya as a whole, the comparatively truncated values for the adjacent cohorts and their ratios, and the adjusted B_{60}s that measure the trends. In countries where nearly all conceptions occur within marriage, the B_{60} from marriage to first birth provides useful information, but in Kenya, as is common in sub-Saharan Africa, the configurations are more complicated. There are too many records in which the reported date of marriage is later than the first birth for this index to be meaningful. The B_{60}s are presented for the parity progressions from the first to second births up to the ninth to the tenth in tabular form and also in a series of graphs (see Figure 4A-1). The numbers of women in many of the individual birth order-cohort cells are relatively small. Sample and bias errors can be appreciable. Interpretation of the trends must be based on the overall pattern rather than specific indices. Nevertheless, the results are quite clear. The B_{60} level is close to 90 percent at low birth orders for the oldest cohort (45-49 years), falling to 80 percent for progressions from five to eight children with a further decrease thereafter. There are distinct, although erratic, declines for younger cohorts in nearly all the progressions, the most doubtful being the fifth to the sixth and the seventh to the eighth. Perhaps the most notable finding is the decrease for the younger cohorts in the B_{60}s at low birth order, even for the movement from first to second. Because most of the women had already attained these births by the time of the survey, the scope for estimation error is small.

To exhibit the trends more effectively, Table 4-7 has been constructed. Here B_{60}s for adjacent parity progressions have been combined to reduce the effects of erratic errors. The slightly anomalous feature of the trend pattern is the apparent modesty of the reductions at the fifth to the seventh births compared to those at higher and lower birth orders by age. This pattern may be an aberrant finding, but it is not necessarily so. The behavioral changes producing the declines in parity progressions are influenced by cohort, time period, and family size factors that may not combine to give strict regularity of trends. Calculations of the ages of mothers at which the

TABLE 4-7   Cumulated B_{60}s from KDHS by Age Group

Age Group	Parity Progression			
	1-3	3-5	5-7	7-9
20-24	.7037	.4325	—	—
25-29	.7611	.6751	.6261	—
30-34	.7713	.7339	.5471	.4080
35-39	.7941	.7589	.6161	.5036
40-44	.7969	.7721	.6521	.5526
45-49	.8133	.8108	.6498	.5955

births of different orders took place show that the time period is displaced roughly 5 years later for each column of the table. Thus, the measures along downward diagonals are approximately for the same time periods, for example, progression one to three for the cohort aged 30-34 years, three to five for 35-39 years, five to seven for 40-44 years, and seven to nine for 45-49 years. The progressions are consistent with the previous conclusion that there was little change in fertility up to some 10 to 15 years before the KDHS but a strong reduction thereafter. Furthermore, the reduction was considerable at all birth orders, although the measures are not sufficiently precise for the exact pattern to be determined.

COMPARISON OF THE PATTERN OF
FERTILITY DECLINE IN KENYA WITH OTHER POPULATIONS

Examination of the pattern of change of the parity progression characteristics of Kenya becomes more significant when comparisons are made with other populations. Juarez (1983, 1987) has presented calculations of B_{60}s from KFS data for several Latin American countries. Brass and Juarez (1983) provided similar results for four Southeast Asian countries. The same methods were applied to the Demographic and Health Survey data for 10 countries of sub-Saharan Africa (other than Kenya) for the present study (Botswana, Burundi, Ghana, Liberia, Mali, Nigeria, Senegal, Togo, Uganda, and Zimbabwe). The interest here is in the trends of parity progression at different orders. To illustrate these as clearly as possible, the progressions have again been combined in adjacent pairs, as in Table 4-7 for Kenya, and expressed relative to the level for the cohort of women aged 45-49 years. The measures for Burundi, Ghana, Liberia, Mali, and Uganda do not suggest that these populations experienced a significant, systematic reduction in fertility in the period prior to the survey. Only the calculations for Burundi are shown as an example, along with the trends for the countries where evidence of change is impressive. The relative progressions for these seven sets of data are given in Table 4-8A.

The downward trends in the parity progressions for Zimbabwe are very similar to those for Kenya but are even more pronounced at the lower birth orders. Equivalent remarks can be made about the Nigerian measures, but the reductions are just as large at the higher birth orders. The Botswana fertility declines are larger still, but it should be noted that the sample sizes for this country were very small. For example, only 87 women aged 45-49 years recorded a second birth, and 33 a seventh, for Botswana compared to 343 and 241, respectively, in the Kenya survey. The very low measures for the relative parity progressions in Botswana for the first to third and third to fifth births in the youngest age groups of women must be treated with great caution. Nevertheless the evidence is convincing that in Botswana, Nigeria,

TABLE 4-8A   Cumulated B_{60}s (relative to 1,000) from KDHS by Age Group for Cohort Aged 45-49:   Africa

Age Group	Parity Progression				Parity Progression			
	1-3	3-5	5-7	7-9	1-3	3-5	5-7	7-9
	Botswana, 1988				Senegal, 1986			
20-24	478				932			
25-29	756	507			998	811		
30-34	938	726	797		1,044	967	864	
35-39	1,012	894	765	703	1,022	945	911	867
40-44	1,054	929	970	767	992	949	923	985
45-49	1,000	1,000	1,000	1,000	1,000	1,000	1,000	1,000
	Burundi, 1987				Togo, 1988			
20-24	1,047				851			
25-29	1,109	952			870	962		
30-34	1,046	1,080	1,013		940	889	760	
35-39	1,074	956	1,014	1,093	938	978	792	1,060
40-44	1,005	967	986	851	946	981	870	1,011
45-49	1,000	1,000	1,000	1,000	1,000	1,000	1,000	1,000
	Kenya, 1988-1989				Zimbabwe, 1988-1989			
20-24	866				813			
25-29	936	832			868	704		
30-34	948	904	841		892	843	857	
35-39	987	935	949	845	970	939	909	974
40-44	979	952	1,003	928	958	972	946	1,080
45-49	1,000	1,000	1,000	1,000	1,000	1,000	1,000	1,000
	Nigeria, 1990							
20-24	781							
25-29	881	821						
30-34	941	859	792					
35-39	964	898	905	793				
40-44	976	944	929	768				
45-49	1,000	1,000	1,000	1,000				

and Zimbabwe, as in Kenya, the reductions in fertility were spread over all parities in the period 10-15 years before the surveys.   The findings for Senegal and Togo are less clear.   There are strong signs of decreases in the parity progressions over cohorts for both countries, but the features are erratic and inconsistent.   The declines in Senegal hardly extended to the lower birth orders and are more irregular than for Kenya, Zimbabwe, and Nigeria.   The measures for Togo are even more uneven, with little reduction at middle (three to five births) and high (seven to nine) orders.   Although the conclusion that there have been declines in parity-dependent fertility seems justified, there must be doubts about the mechanisms of change.

Table 4-8B presents comparable measures derived from World Fertility Survey (WFS) data for Latin American and Southeast Asian populations (Juarez 1983, 1987; Brass and Juarez, 1983). For Peru, Panama, and Paraguay the B_{60}s are calculated only up to the sixth birth. The fifth to seventh progression is, therefore, replaced in the table by the fourth to sixth to retain a two-birth interval only slightly displaced from the majority classification. In interpreting the trends, it should be remembered that birth histories are snapshots of the fertility expression at points of time and do not in

TABLE 4-8B   Cumulated B_{60}s (relative to 1,000) from KFS by Age Group for Cohort Aged 45-49: Latin American and Asia

Age Group	Parity Progression				Parity Progression			
	1-3	3-5	5-7	7-9	1-3	3-5	5-7	7-9
	Colombia, 1976				Panama, 1975[a]			
25-29	812	591			915			
30-34	949	731	627		984	714	686	
35-39	980	847	773	676	1,047	956	916	
40-44	967	983	933	794	1,067	988	837	
45-49	1,000	1,000	1,000	1,000	1,000	1,000	1,000	
	Costa Rica, 1976				Paraguay, 1979[a]			
25-29	630	520			745			
30-34	801	723	513		876	871	781	
35-39	900	856	741	765	892	813	790	
40-44	966	1,003	898	952	997	910	924	
45-49	1,000	1,000	1,000	1,000	1,000	1,000	1,000	
	Mexico, 1976-1977				Peru, 1977-1978[a]			
25-29	985	813			968			
30-34	998	899	895	834	975	828	908	
35-39	1,054	973	954	850	1,040	859	949	
40-44	1,009	1,040	1,022	892	1,024	903	970	
45-49	1,000	1,000	1,000	1,000	1,000	1,000	1,000	
	Korea, 1974				Sri Lanka, 1975			
25-29	1,076				898	671		
30-34	1,089	542			938	740	741	
35-39	1,091	648	535		1,005	837	928	821
40-44	1,041	911	738	654	993	926	928	897
45-49	1,000	1,000	1,000	1,000	1,000	1,000	1,000	1,000

[a]Fourth to sixth births.

general correspond to the same stage of development in each case. For the present purpose of comparison with the African changes as recorded in the late 1980s, it is desirable that the initiation of fertility declines should have been some 10 to 15 years before the survey. It is fortuitous, but convenient, that this criterion is roughly met by most of the WFS data sets for Latin America and Asia that are the basis of Table 4-8B. The parity progressions from the WFS for the Dominican Republic in 1975, Pakistan in 1975, and Nepal in 1976 are not shown, because there was no evidence of decline.

The typical trend pattern displayed in Table 4-8B is of initial movements downward at moderate parity progressions (three to four, and four to five). Reductions at higher parities are generally somewhat later and smaller. The extension to lower birth orders (one to two, and two to three) occurs more slowly and may lag considerably as, for example, in Mexico, Peru, and Korea where little, if any, reduction was achieved in the progression from the first to the third birth by the time of the WFS. Nearly all the countries conform well with this typical pattern, although there are uncertainties due to sample fluctuations and the truncation at higher parities, particularly for Paraguay. The most notable exception is Costa Rica where the declines in the parity progressions at the third to the fifth births were matched by the declines at higher and lower orders, such as occurred in Kenya, Zimbabwe, and Nigeria. However, the reductions were much larger in Costa Rica, and the fertility transition was probably at a more advanced stage. The configurations of change in the African countries during the 1980s are not demonstrably unique but are certainly unusual in comparison with the Latin American and Asian experience.

DIFFERENTIALS IN THE PATTERNS OF FERTILITY DECLINE

The B_{60}s for provinces, residence, and educational groups are displayed in Tables 4-9A, 4-9B, and 4-9C. Because of the relatively small numbers, the parities are amalgamated further to show progressions only from the first to the fourth and the fourth to the seventh births. For Kenya as a whole, the downward trend over cohorts for the first to the fourth progression is strongly established, but for the fourth to the seventh it is rather modest, although apparent. This pattern is in conformity with the comments made earlier made about the fifth to the seventh birth progression. The measures for the subpopulations confirm that the fertility reductions contain a strong component of declines in family building and are not due primarily to changes in populations at risk.

The variations among subpopulations cannot be traced with any precision because of the erratic consequences of the small numbers, and reference will be made only to the most notable. The steep trend downward in Central Province for both low and moderate birth orders is evident. The

TABLE 4-9A Cumulated B_{60}s from KDHS by Age Group—by Province for Parity Progressions One to Four and Four to Seven

Age Group	Kenya		Nairobi		Central		Coast	
	1-4	4-7	1-4	4-7	1-4	4-7	1-4	4-7
20-24	.5022	—	.4617	—	.5553	—	.6743	—
25-29	.6152	.5230	.2836	—	.5190	.2356	.5434	.3602
30-34	.6631	.4670	.4015	.1780	.7214	.2736	.6424	.5089
35-39	.6935	.5354	.4534	.2806	.6712	.4849	.6538	.4912
40-44	.7187	.5596	.5244	.2326	.7539	.5786	.7708	.6713
45-49	.7326	.5849	.6000	.2084	.6817	.4694	.5663	.5892

	Nyanza		Rift		Western		Eastern	
	1-4	4-7	1-4	4-7	1-4	4-7	1-4	4-7
20-24	.6631	—	.4757	—	.8207	—	.4321	—
25-29	.7123	.4729	.5790	—	.8192	—	.6824	—
30-34	.7199	.5783	.5434	.3410	.8670	.7002	.6882	.5933
35-39	.7415	.6039	.6867	.4820	.7930	.6274	.6980	.6106
40-44	.7019	.6307	.7064	.4968	.7172	.5986	.7432	.5600
45-49	.8500	.7163	.7112	.4906	.7949	.6596	.7253	.6633

TABLE 4-9B Cumulated B_{60}s from KDHS by Age Group—by Residence for Parity Progressions One to Four and Four to Seven

Age Group	Urban		Rural	
	1-4	4-7	1-4	4-7
20-24	.4382	—	.5373	—
25-29	.3305	—	.6775	.5693
30-34	.4158	.2506	.7133	.4934
35-39	.4788	.3437	.7235	.5900
40-44	.5146	.2626	.7394	.5811
45-49	.6300	.3248	.7412	.6038

only province for which there are not well-established reductions in parity progressions is Western. In contrast, there are indications of increases for younger cohorts, which add further doubts about the reliability of the data. Of course, there are determinants that could have altered to produce the configuration. The most obvious possibilities are reductions in secondary sterility and shorter periods of lactation. Neither appears very plausible in

TABLE 4-9C Cumulated B_{60}s from KDHS by Age Group—by Education for Parity Progressions One to Four and Four to Seven

Age Group	No Schooling		1-4 Years	
	1-4	4-7	1-4	4-7
20-24	.6018	—	.5176	—
25-29	.6691	.4304	.6492	—
30-34	.6671	.5536	.7465	.5008
35-39	.7148	.5721	.7530	.5938
40-44	.6750	.5903	.7993	.5749
45-49	.6966	.5965	.8511	.6240
	5-8 Years		9+ Years	
	1-4	4-7	1-4	4-7
20-24	.5383	—	.3352	—
25-29	.5513	—	.4204	—
30-34	.7200	.4314	.4406	.1862
35-39	.6207	.4967	.3957	.4408
40-44	.7979	.5043	.4590	.4363
45-49	.7795	.4669	.4243	.3918

such a high-fertility subpopulation, since the magnitude of the biological changes would have to be large to produce more than a marginal effect.

In both Nairobi and the urban areas as a whole, there appears to be little if any downward trend at moderate parities, but the cautions already given about interpretation of the fertility measures for these subpopulations apply. The parity progressions for educational categories are again in line with expectations based on the comparison between the birth rates in the 5 years preceding the KDHS and the KFS. The downward trends are very similar for the subgroups. Again the distinct declines for the residual category of women with no schooling are particularly noteworthy. The picture that emerges from the examination of the B_{60}s for Kenya and its subpopulations is in close agreement with results from the comparison of measures of fertility by subgroups in 1973-1977 and 1984-1988. As pointed out, the former analysis is focused on changes in family building that are little influenced by alterations in the populations at risk. Nor are biological proximate determinants significant factors in parity progression changes, except possibly for secondary sterility. The near universality of the trends over subpopulations suggests that change in sterility is an unlikely explanation. The most plausible reason for the parity progression reduction is the increased use of contraception.[2] It is also important to bear in mind that these calculations are based on birth records for cohorts collected at one survey, the KDHS, and are thus insensitive to data errors due to possible lack of comparability in the procedures and efficiency of the two surveys, the KFS and KDHS. The consistency of the findings from the two approaches is a cogent argument for their essential validity.

FERTILITY DECLINES BY DISTRICT

The declines in fertility show distinct regional differences, but the provinces are not sufficiently homogeneous to be accepted as the most effective aggregates for the study of patterns. Unfortunately, the information for analysis at the district level is limited by the sample sizes of the KFS and the KDHS. When tabulations from the 1989 census of women by age and the number of children born to them are available by district, it will be possible to compare the measures with the corresponding data from the 1979 census. Although problems from the underreporting of births in the censuses by the older women will still remain, it is probable that satisfactory allowances can be made and the trends estimated. The direct measures of current fertility based on the census reports of births in the preceding year are subject to substantial error and cannot be used without adjustments. The fertility declines in Kenya between the two censuses should be large enough for the effects to be evident in the mean parities, although the magnitudes of these cohort changes will not be the same as for the time-period movements.

In the KDHS there was some oversampling to provide larger numbers of households in selected districts. Tabulations of births by age group of women and 5-year calendar periods have been made for the 16 districts with the largest sample sizes. The smallest group included is 167 women for Nakuru; the largest excluded, 111 for Kiambu. Nairobi has already been included among the provinces in earlier analysis. Our evaluation of birth reporting at the KDHS concluded that the fertility calculated for the period 10 to 14 years before the survey was in close agreement with the corresponding measure from the 5 years preceding the KFS. Accordingly, the change at the district level is estimated from the comparison of the cumulated rates for women up to age 40 in the 5 years preceding the KDHS with those from 10-14 years before. The upper limit of 40 years is necessary because of the truncation of maternity histories with increasing time in the past.

---

[2]The role of contraceptive use as a proximate determinant of Kenyan fertility is examined more thoroughly in the next chapter.

Table 4-10 presents the percentage declines in fertility as measured for selected districts and also for provinces. For the latter, the reductions found previously from the comparison of KDHS and KFS estimates (Tables 4-6A to 4-6C) are given in the last column and can be compared to KDHS estimates in the first column. The bases of the two sets of province indices differ in the age ranges of women (less than 40 and up to 50 years), as well as the source and calendar period of the earlier fertility measure (1974-1978 from the KDHS and 1973-1977 from the KFS). Nevertheless the agreement is rather satisfactory except for Nairobi. The discrepancy for the capital is probably due to the less stable nature of the population, leading to both erratic change and reporting errors. In Central, Coast, Eastern, and Western provinces, the fertility declines calculated solely from KDHS data are a few percentage points lower than the corresponding values from the KDHS-KFS comparison, and for Nyanza and Rift Valley slightly above.

The agreement at the province level confirms that the measures of district change based on KDHS alone are valid, but the problem of sample variability remains. To provide some check, the changes in fertility from 5-9 years prior to the KDHS to 0-4 years before for women under 45 were also calculated and are shown in the middle column of the table. The estimates from the two series are not, of course, independent but provide a useful guide to the possible existence of major anomalies. The results are, generally, satisfyingly consistent. On average, the fertility declines from 1979-1983 to 1984-1988 were about two-thirds the corresponding percentages of 1974-1978 to 1984-1988. The largest discrepancies are for Kirinyaga, Kisii, and Uasin Gishu, where the second series suggests that the already large fertility decreases may have been underestimated, and for Bungoma and Kisumu where increases are indicated rather than small reductions. Thus the relative order of the changes is little affected. The one exception is Mombasa where a moderately large fertility decline in the first series becomes a small one in the second. The correlation coefficient between the rankings of the two series (Kendall's) is .68, which indicates a strong association.

The selected districts in the Coast and Rift Valley record fertility declines that are close to the overall measures for their provinces. The district variations in Central Province are greater, although all the reductions are substantial; the 36.5 percent reduction for Kirinyaga is the largest of all the declines. In Nyanza, the fertility decrease of 13.5 percent conceals two small reductions in Kisumu and South Nyanza, as well as two large ones in Kisii and Siaya. The differential for Kisii is not particularly surprising because the district has several characteristics, including ethnic composition, that distinguish it from the rest of Nyanza; the result for Siaya is, however, unexpected. The two selected districts of Western Province have

TABLE 4-10 Declines in Cumulated Fertility by Province and District

Province and District	Decline (%)		
	1974-1978 to 1984-1988 Women Under 40 Years[a]	1979-1983 to 1984-1988 Women Under 45 Years[a]	1973-1977 to 1984-1988 Women Under 50 Years[b]
Central	26.7	21.4	31
Kirinyaga	36.5	33.5	
Muranga	20.6	12.4	
Nyeri	24.2	18.6	
Coast	21.0	22.6	27
Kilifi	19.3	15.7	
Mombasa	19.8	5.2	
Eastern	13.3	12.1	16
Machakos	11.8	6.9	
Meru	21.7	15.1	
Nyanza	13.5	8.4	13
Kisii	19.3	18.9	
Kisumu	6.6	-1.2	
Siaya	27.4	18.5	
South Nyanza	6.6	6.3	
Rift Valley	22.8	16.2	20
Kericho	22.3	11.4	
Nakuru	23.3	18.7	
Uasin Gishu	25.8	22.6	
Western	1.3	-1.8	5
Bungoma	8.1	-4.8	
Kakamega	10.2	4.8	
Nairobi	14.0	9.1	26

[a]Estimated from births in time periods reported in the KDHS.
[b]Estimated from births reported in the five years prior to the KDHS and KFS.

small fertility declines, and the province measure is even lower, implying that such is the case for the one district excluded, Busia.

The selected districts comprise 17 of the 41 total but include more than two-thirds of the Kenyan population. Many of the excluded areas are geographically remote from the central area and are thinly populated, but those characteristics do not make their fertility changes less interesting—rather, the contrary is true. In particular, the results for Coast Province demonstrate that the declines for the districts not selected must on average have been a little greater than the overall provincial measure of 21 percent to balance the 19.3 percent for Kilifi and 19.8 percent for Mombasa. Of the remaining districts, three (Kwale, Lamu, and Tana River) have typical Coast Province features of low educational level and high child mortality with little improvement; the other, Taita, does not conform to these characteristics but includes only one-quarter of the population of the selected districts and slightly more than one-tenth of the province as a whole.

A further check was applied by comparing the mean parities by age groups of women for the selected districts at the 1988-1989 KDHS with corresponding measures from the 1979 census. There is clear evidence of the underreporting of births by older women in 1979, but the mean parities for younger women are close on average to measures from the 1977-1978 KFS. Another reason for omitting the older women in the comparisons is the fact that a considerable proportion of their births took place before the fertility decline was clearly established. After investigation it was decided that only the first four 5-year age groups (i.e., 15-34 years) should be retained to provide a measure of fertility as a sum of the mean parities. Various alternative systems of weighing the mean parities were examined, but the resulting changes in the estimates of fertility declines from the 1979 census to the 1988-1989 KDHS were too small to justify the added complication.

Table 4-11 gives the ratios of the fertility index from the 1988-1989 KDHS to the 1979 census for provinces and the selected districts. These are generally slightly lower than the measures presented earlier, probably because of relative underreporting of births at the census, but in Nyanza the discrepancy is in the opposite direction. The possible effects of age misstatements and sample errors should not be forgotten. It is arguable whether adjustments for the presumed birth reporting errors at the 1979 census should be made for districts, but on balance, their use seems to improve the measures of change. The adjustment made assumes that the proportional discrepancy between the 1979 census and the 1977-1978 KFS for a province also applies to districts in the province. The adjusted ratios are then translated into percentage declines in the fertility index. The last column repeats for comparison the district fertility reduction between 1974-1978 and 1984-1988 calculated from the KDHS birth histories. The province divergences

TABLE 4-11   Declines in Fertility Indices by Province and District

Province and District	Mean Parity Index Ratios 1988 1989 KDHS to 1979 Census (per thousand)			Cumulated Fertility Reduction 1974-1978 to 1984-1988 from KDHS (%)
	Reported	Adjusted	Reduction Based on Adjusted %	
Central	889	879	12.1	26.7
Kirinyaga	815	806	19.4	36.5
Muranga	848	839	16.1	20.6
Nyeri	901	891	10.9	24.2
Coast	889	847	15.3	21.0
Kilifi	890	848	15.2	19.3
Mombasa	882	840	16.0	19.8
Eastern	904	898	10.2	13.3
Machakos	881	875	12.5	11.8
Meru	920	914	8.6	21.7
Nyanza	911	959	4.1	13.5
Kisii	830	874	12.6	19.3
Kisumu	854	899	10.1	6.6
Siaya	1,035	1,090	−9.0	27.4
S. Nyanza	916	964	3.6	6.6
Rift Valley	925	893	10.7	22.8
Kericho	980	946	5.4	22.3
Nakuru	666	643	35.7	23.3
Uasin Gishu	908	877	12.3	25.8
Western	981	951	4.9	1.3
Bungoma	969	939	6.1	8.1
Kakamega	985	955	4.5	10.2
Nairobi	915	759	24.1	14.0

(reported to adjusted) are only around 1 percent in Central and Eastern provinces, and 3 percent in Rift Valley and Western, but rise to 5 percent in Coast and Nyanza. The disagreement for Nairobi is much larger, but there are particular problems of obtaining accurate reports from this fluid population.

As already noted, the declines in the mean parity index are not measuring the same effects as the direct time-period reductions. There should, however, be a reasonably consistent relationship. If Nairobi is excluded, the decreases in the mean parity index are overall roughly three-fifths of the change in the direct time-period fertility measures. For individual provinces there is a moderate fluctuation about this relation but no striking anomaly. The adjusted mean parity decline for Nairobi is well above the expected value, but the unadjusted is considerably below. Discrepancies at the district level are greater than at the province level in accord with expectation, but the general order of the fertility declines is largely preserved. Thus, Nakuru and Kisumu record substantially greater fertility reductions in the mean parity ratios than in the time-period measures, but in the former case the shift is from high to the highest and in the latter from the lowest to moderately low. The divergences for Kericho and Machakos are of more concern because the former ranks well up for fertility reduction by the direct time-period measurement but near the lowest for the mean parity ratio, and the shift for the latter district is the reverse. The most striking anomaly of all is for Siaya, which shows the second highest decline in the cumulated fertility measure but a rise in mean parities (whether adjusted or not). It is clear that care has to be exercised in drawing conclusions about fertility change for these districts in which the evidence is contradictory.

SUMMARY

The evidence from censuses and surveys indicates that fertility fell in the late 1970s and the 1980s, probably with a more rapid rate of decline in the late 1980s. Total fertility decreased from approximately 8.2 births per woman in 1973-1977 to 6.7 births per woman in 1984-1988. The decline was notable in that it occurred in almost every subgroup. All age groups contributed to the decline, with the middle and later reproductive ages contributing the most. Fertility declined 23 percent in urban areas, followed closely by a decrease of 17 percent in rural areas. The greatest fertility reduction among the provinces occurred in Central Province (31 percent). The fertility decline in Coast Province, noted for its substantial Muslim population, was also high (27 percent). Western Province was an anomaly, with a small decline of only 5 percent, which may be more a result of the data than a reflection of what actually occurred. Fertility reductions in percentage terms were very similar regardless of women's educational level.

Fertility declines occurred at all birth orders, a pattern that is very different from that observed in Latin America and Asia, where fertility declines started in the middle parities and moved successively to the higher and then lower birth orders (see Caldwell et al., 1992, for related discussion on the differences of fertility declines in Africa). An analysis of the patterns of decline among other sub-Saharan African countries revealed a pattern similar to Kenya in those countries experiencing fertility change.

APPENDIX

TABLE 4A-1   The Proportion of Women Progressing to the Next Birth Within 5 Years, KDHS, All Women

	Parity Progression			
	1st-2nd	2nd-3rd	3rd-4th	4th-5th
B_{60} unadjusted				
Cohort age				
15-19	.9246	1.0000	.5625	.0000
20-24	.8744	.8832	.8122	.5952
25-29	.8926	.8975	.8638	.8697
30-34	.8747	.9081	.8907	.8893
35-39	.9056	.8934	.8877	.8818
40-44	.8966	.8961	.9049	.8598
45-49	.9121	.8917	.9008	.9001
Cohort age (5 years later)				
20-24[a]	.8808	.5362	.2779	.0000
25-29[a]	.9080	.9198	.9199	.8203
30-34[a]	.8762	.9264	.9188	.8889
35-39[a]	.9082	.9005	.9048	.9052
40-44[a]	.8974	.9047	.9167	.8688
45-49[a]	.9137	.8975	.9038	.9039
Indices of relative change				
20-24/25-29[a]	0.9630	0.9602		
25-29/30-34[a]	1.0187	0.9687	0.9402	.9783
30-34/35-39[a]	0.9631	1.0085	0.9844	.9824
35-39/40-44[a]	1.0091	0.9875	0.9684	1.0149
40-44/45-49[a]	0.9813	0.9985	1.0012	.9512
B_{60} adjusted				
20-24	.8533	.8247		
25-29	.8861	.8589	.8083	.8352
30-34	.8699	.8866	.8597	.8537
35-39	.9032	.8792	.8733	.8690
40-44	.8951	.8903	.9018	.8562
45-49	.9121	.8917	.9008	.9001

continued

TABLE 4A-1   *Continued*

	Parity Progression				
	5th-6th	6th-7th	7th-8th	8th-9th	9th-10th
B_{60} unadjusted					
Cohort age					
15-19	.0000	.0000	.0000	.0000	.0000
20-24	1.0000	.0000	.0000	.0000	.0000
25-29	.9180	.9093	.8549	.3388	.0000
30-34	.8620	.8076	.8980	.7195	.6169
35-39	.8321	.8557	.8266	.8086	.8342
40-44	.8777	.7966	.7955	.7874	.7094
45-49	.8174	.7950	.8018	.7427	.6763
Cohort age (5 years later)					
20-24[a]	.0000	.0000	.0000	.0000	.0000
25-29[a]	.4302	.1417	.0000	.0000	.0000
30-34[a]	.8713	.8370	1.0000	.8769	.4020
35-39[a]	.8484	.9241	.8362	.9540	.7319
40-44[a]	.9005	.8369	.8771	.8361	.8164
45-49[a]	.8303	.8391	.8202	.8231	.7891
Indices of relative change					
20-24/25-29[a]					
25-29/30-34[a]	1.0536	1.0864			
30-34/35-39[a]	1.0160	0.8739	1.0740	0.7542	0.8428
35-39/40-44[a]	0.9240	1.0224	0.9424	0.9670	1.0218
40-44/45-49[a]	1.0570	0.9494	0.9699	0.9567	0.8989
B_{60} adjusted					
15-19					
20-24					
25-29	.8546	.7326			
30-34	.8112	.6744	.7871	.5183	.5236
35-39	.7984	.7717	.7329	.6871	.6213
40-44	.8640	.7548	.7777	.7106	.6080
45-49	.8174	.7950	.8018	.7427	.6763

[a]Truncated to give the same age range of births as for the next lower age group.

First to Second Birth

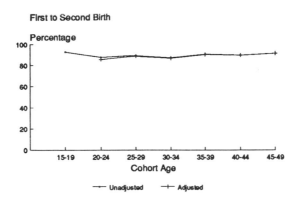

Second to Third Birth

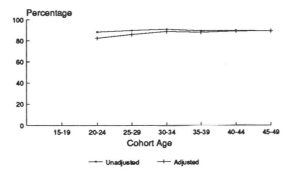

Third to Fourth Birth

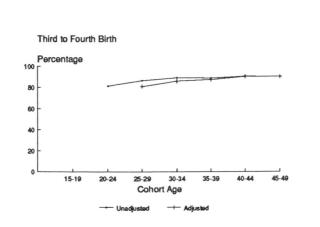

continued

FIGURE 4A-1   Unadjusted and adjusted B_{60}s for the parity progressions.

Fourth to Fifth Birth

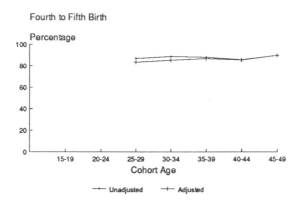

Fifth to Sixth Birth

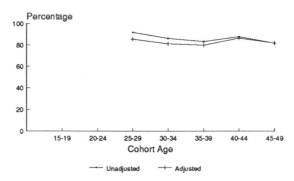

Sixth to Seventh Birth

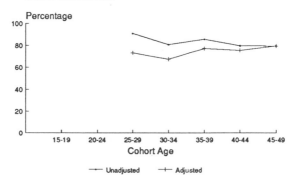

FIGURE 4A-1   *Continued*

Seventh to Eighth Birth

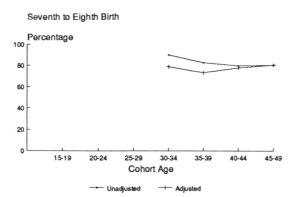

Eighth to Ninth Birth

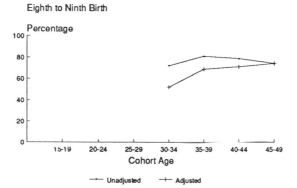

Ninth to Tenth Birth

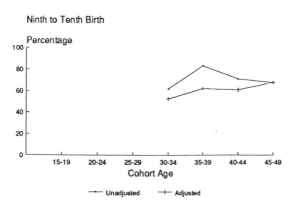

FIGURE 4A-1   *Continued*

5

Proximate Determinants of Fertility

From the analysis in Chapter 4, it is clear that fertility declined substantially between the times of the Kenya Fertility Survey (KFS, 1977-1978) and Kenya Demographic and Health Survey (KDHS, 1988-1989). This chapter takes a closer look at the proximate determinants that contributed to this decline by using the Bongaarts framework to quantify the effects on fertility of marriage patterns, contraception, postpartum infecundability, primary sterility, and abortion.

FRAMEWORK

Bongaarts et al. (1984) enumerated nine proximate determinants of fertility:

1. percentage of women in sexual union,
2. frequency of sexual intercourse,
3. postpartum abstinence,
4. lactational amenorrhea,
5. contraceptive use,
6. induced abortion,
7. spontaneous intrauterine mortality,
8. natural sterility, and
9. pathological sterility.

These factors are the behavioral and biological factors that influence fertility directly. Cultural, psychological, economic, social, health, and environmental factors affect fertility indirectly through these proximate determinants.

Bongaarts and Potter (1983) quantified the effects of six of the nine proximate determinants of fertility that were shown to have the greatest effect on fertility in 41 populations: percentage of women in sexual union, postpartum abstinence and lactational amenorrhea (taken together), contraceptive use, abortion, and pathological sterility. They summarized the effect of each determinant on fertility in an index, which generally ranges from 0 to 1, with 0 having the greatest inhibiting effect on fertility and 1 having the least inhibiting effect (i.e., the lower the index, the more it reduces fertility). Each index (not equal to 1) reduces the total fecundity rate (TF), which is the level of fertility expected in the absence of any of the nine proximate determinants outlined above. Of course, no one knows what TF really is, but Bongaarts and Potter (1983) estimated that it ranges from 13 to 17, with an average of approximately 15. Below is a description of each of the proximate determinants used in this analysis and how they affect fertility. The computational procedures used to estimate each index are described in the appendix to this chapter.

Percentage of Women in Sexual Union

It is assumed that the number of women of reproductive age married or living with someone determines the proportion of women in a society exposed to the risk of becoming pregnant. The greater the number of women exposed, the higher is the resulting fertility. In sub-Saharan Africa, entry into union[1] has generally occurred at an early age, and although union dissolution is frequent in many regions, remarriage occurs rapidly (Cochrane and Farid, 1989). Kenya has been no exception to this general pattern. Table 5-1 shows the median age at first union for women 20 to 49 years. In 1977-1978 the median age at first union at the national level was 17.5 years. At the province level, Coast Province had the lowest age at first union, 16.4; followed closely by Nyanza, 16.5; and Western, 16.8. As expected, Nairobi had the highest age at first union, 19.1; with Central, 18.8, and Eastern, 18.7, not far behind.

Results from the KDHS show that age at first marriage has risen across all provinces, ranging from an increase of 0.4 year for Nyanza to 1.1 years for Nairobi, Central, and Western provinces. At the national level, age at

---

[1]In this report, the terms marriage and union are used interchangeably. Because entry into marriage may be a process not just a single event, and because a woman may live with a man without being formally married, this analysis looks at the effect of the proportions of women in sexual union, rather than marriage per se, on fertility.

TABLE 5-1   Median Age at First Marriage[a] Among Women Age 20-49 by Subgroup, 1977-1978 KFS and 1988-1989 KDHS (years)

Subgroup	KFS Total	KDHS - Age at Time of Survey						KDHS Total
		20-24	25-29	30-34	35-39	40-44	45-49	
National	17.5	19.8	18.6	17.9	17.9	17.3	18.5	18.5
Residence								
Rural	17.4	19.7	18.3	17.7	17.8	17.3	18.4	18.3
Urban	18.1	20.3	19.9	19.6	18.7	18.7	19.5	19.8
Province								
Nairobi	19.1	20.5	20.1	19.9	19.5	19.4	22.6	20.2
Central	18.8	21.9	20.1	19.3	19.3	18.2	19.1	19.9
Coast	16.4	19.5	17.1	16.3	16.2	15.1	16.3	17.0
Eastern	18.7	22.5	19.2	20.0	19.1	18.3	18.9	19.5
Nyanza	16.5	17.7	17.1	16.4	16.6	16.4	17.1	16.9
Rift Valley	17.5	19.3	17.6	17.2	18.3	17.3	20.4	18.1
Western	16.8	19.0	18.5	17.7	17.1	16.9	15.4	17.9

[a]The age by which 50 percent of women have entered their first union.

first union increased by one year to 18.5. Among other sub-Saharan African populations, where the Demographic and Health Surveys (DHS) were conducted, age at first union ranges from 15.7 in Mali to 19.7 in Ondo State, Nigeria, placing Kenya toward the upper end of these two extremes. Furthermore, there are other indications that age at first union is increasing in Kenya; younger women are marrying at older ages. As indicated in Table 5-1, for women age 20 to 24 the median age at first union in 1989 was 19.8 years.

The index measuring the effect of marriage patterns on fertility is denoted as C_m. It takes the value of 1 when all women of reproductive age are in union and 0 when none are in union.

Contraception

Use of contraception to delay or limit the number of children born clearly affects a society's fertility level. Historically, contraceptive use in sub-Saharan Africa, including Kenya, has been very low. However, substantial increases in the use of contraception have been identified in Kenya, Botswana, and Zimbabwe on the basis of data from the DHS (Jolly and Gribble, 1993; Working Group on Factors Affecting Contraceptive Use, 1993).

Tables 5-2 and 5-3 show contraceptive prevalence rates by subgroup and specific method used for Kenya at the times of the KFS and the KDHS, respectively. In 1977-1978, contraceptive use was very low, with only 5.6

TABLE 5-2 Women Currently in Union Using Contraception by Subgroup, 1977-1978 KFS (percent)

Subgroup	Any Method	Pill	IUD	Injection	Vaginal Methods	Condom	Female Sterilization	Periodic Abstinence	Withdrawal	Other
National	5.6	2.0	0.7	0.6	0.0	0.1	0.9	1.1	1.1	0.0
15-24	3.9	2.0	0.2	0.1	0.0	0.2	0.0	1.2	0.1	0.1
25-34	6.6	2.6	0.9	0.7	0.0	0.1	0.9	1.2	0.1	0.1
35-49	5.9	1.4	0.8	0.8	0.1	0.1	1.4	0.9	0.2	0.2
Residence										
Rural	4.7	1.6	0.5	0.5	0.0	0.1	0.8	1.1	0.1	0.0
Urban	11.6	5.1	1.9	1.4	0.0	0.2	1.4	1.3	0.2	0.1
Education										
None	3.2	0.7	0.4	0.3	0.0	0.1	0.7	0.8	0.2	0.0
1-4 years	5.4	1.3	0.8	0.9	0.1	0.1	0.7	1.5	0.0	0.0
5-7 years	7.5	3.4	0.7	0.6	0.0	0.2	0.8	1.2	0.3	0.3
8+ years	18.4	9.6	2.6	1.4	0.0	0.5	2.5	1.8	0.0	0.0
Parity										
0	1.1	0.1	0.0	0.0	0.0	0.0	0.5	0.3	0.0	0.2
1	2.4	1.2	0.1	0.0	0.0	0.2	0.0	0.8	0.0	0.1
2	4.7	2.5	0.4	0.0	0.0	0.3	0.5	0.9	0.0	0.1
3	5.6	2.4	0.3	0.2	0.0	0.0	0.6	1.6	0.3	0.2
4+	7.0	2.2	1.1	1.0	0.0	0.1	1.2	1.2	0.2	0.0
Province										
Nairobi	15.9	7.3	2.6	2.1	0.0	0.1	2.0	1.5	0.0	0.3
Central	9.0	3.3	2.1	1.4	0.0	0.2	0.7	0.9	0.4	0.0
Coast	4.4	1.6	0.3	1.0	0.0	0.0	1.0	0.4	0.1	0.0
Eastern	6.8	2.3	1.2	0.1	0.1	0.6	1.3	0.8	0.4	0.0
Nyanza	3.1	0.9	0.1	0.3	0.0	0.0	0.3	1.5	0.0	0.0
Rift Valley	5.5	1.5	0.1	0.5	0.0	0.0	1.3	1.9	0.2	0.0
Western	2.9	1.5	0.1	0.0	0.0	0.0	0.5	0.1	0.0	0.7

TABLE 5-3 Women Currently in Union Using Contraception by Subgroup, 1988-1989 KDHS (percent)

Subgroup	Any Method	Pill	IUD	Injection	Vaginal Methods	Condom	Female Sterilization	Periodic Abstinence	Withdrawal	Other
National	26.8	5.2	3.7	3.3	0.4	0.5	4.7	7.5	0.2	1.3
15-24	18.4	6.3	2.0	0.9	0.1	0.8	0.5	6.8	0.2	0.8
25-34	28.4	6.7	4.1	4.2	0.4	0.5	3.3	7.4	0.3	1.5
35-49	30.7	2.9	4.4	3.9	0.7	0.2	9.0	8.0	0.2	1.4
Residence										
Rural	26.0	4.3	2.9	3.4	0.4	0.4	4.9	8.1	0.2	1.4
Urban	30.5	9.8	8.0	2.8	0.5	0.8	3.6	4.0	0.4	0.6
Education										
None	18.3	2.1	1.3	2.2	0.1	0.3	3.7	6.9	0.0	1.7
1-4 years	25.5	4.3	2.7	4.3	0.6	0.1	6.0	6.6	0.0	0.9
5-7 years	29.4	6.2	3.5	4.7	0.3	0.3	4.9	7.7	0.4	1.4
8+ years	37.9	9.2	8.8	2.2	1.1	1.4	4.8	9.0	0.6	0.8
Parity										
0	4.6	0.6	0.0	0.2	0.0	0.0	0.0	3.4	0.4	0.0
1	16.8	5.2	1.8	0.7	0.0	0.5	0.3	8.1	0.0	0.2
2	24.2	6.7	4.4	1.6	0.2	1.2	1.9	7.2	0.1	0.9
3	28.4	9.3	3.3	2.4	0.3	0.5	2.7	8.4	0.9	0.6
4+	31.4	4.3	4.4	4.8	0.7	0.4	7.1	7.7	0.1	1.9

Province										
Nairobi	33.6	11.8	7.9	2.3	1.2	0.4	4.4	4.0	0.8	0.8
Central	39.7	8.1	10.0	3.6	0.3	1.3	7.7	7.1	0.3	1.3
Coast	18.1	5.5	1.7	3.6	0.1	0.3	3.6	3.0	0.3	0.0
Eastern	40.1	5.9	4.7	3.5	0.4	0.4	4.5	17.9	0.3	2.5
Nyanza	13.7	2.7	0.8	2.5	0.0	0.3	3.9	3.0	0.0	0.5
Rift Valley	29.6	3.6	2.3	5.3	1.0	0.5	5.5	9.0	0.3	2.1
Western	13.7	3.8	1.6	1.6	0.2	0.2	2.6	3.0	0.0	0.7
District										
Bungoma	9.3	2.7	1.5	0.5	0.0	0.3	1.3	1.1	0.0	1.9
Kakamega	14.9	3.1	1.1	2.3	0.3	0.3	3.8	3.7	0.0	0.3
Kericho	23.1	3.4	0.8	5.3	0.4	0.0	5.3	6.8	0.0	1.1
Kilifi	10.8	4.6	0.6	2.5	0.3	0.3	0.8	1.4	0.3	0.0
Kirinyaga	52.2	12.4	18.6	8.0	0.4	0.9	4.0	7.1	0.4	0.4
Kisii	21.5	2.5	2.0	5.7	0.0	0.4	6.4	4.1	0.0	0.4
Kisumu	17.9	4.8	1.0	3.0	0.0	0.0	5.3	3.5	0.0	0.3
Machakos	40.4	5.3	1.4	1.1	0.0	0.7	3.5	24.5	0.7	3.2
Meru	36.3	12.4	8.3	5.7	1.6	0.5	5.7	2.1	0.0	0.0
Mombasa	24.4	8.8	5.4	2.0	0.0	0.7	4.1	2.7	0.7	0.0
Muranga	33.9	3.8	10.5	3.0	0.4	1.3	7.5	6.6	0.4	0.4
Nakuru	47.1	1.7	5.4	4.9	2.0	1.2	12.7	14.7	0.0	4.5
Nyeri	40.7	9.2	9.1	2.5	0.4	0.8	12.6	5.3	0.4	0.4
Siaya	8.4	0.6	0.0	1.2	0.0	1.2	2.4	2.4	0.0	0.6
South Nyanza	6.1	2.0	0.0	0.0	0.0	0.0	1.4	2.0	0.0	0.7
Uasin Gishu	13.4	3.8	0.5	3.8	0.0	0.0	1.0	3.3	0.5	0.5

percent of all women in a union currently using any method.[2] About one-fourth of the methods used were traditional (periodic abstinence or rhythm, withdrawal, and other). As in many other regions of the world, contraceptive use was higher for women who were living in urban areas and were well educated. Contraceptive use was also greater among women of higher parity. By 1988-1989, use of any method had increased substantially among women in union to 26.8 percent, with about one-third of these women using traditional methods. Contraceptive prevalence remained higher for women who were living in urban areas (30.5 percent), who were well educated (37.9 percent for women with more than 8 years of schooling), and who had given birth to more children (31.4 percent of women with four or more births).

Nairobi, Central, and Eastern provinces had the highest prevalence rates of the provinces at both times. Western and Nyanza had the lowest rates. Among the districts in 1988-1989, contraceptive use was highest in Kirinyaga (52 percent), followed by Nakuru (47.1 percent), Nyeri (40.7 percent), and Machakos (40.4 percent). Siaya and South Nyanza had very low prevalence rates, 8.4 and 6.1 percent, respectively.

The type of contraceptive used also varied by province. The pill was the most commonly used contraceptive in Nairobi, Coast, and Western provinces; sterilization in Nyanza Province; the IUD in Central Province; and periodic abstinence or rhythm in Eastern and Rift Valley provinces.

C_c, the index of contraception, measures the effect on fertility of the proportion of women using contraception, as well as the effectiveness of the methods used: C_c equals 1 if no contraception is used and 0 if all fecund women use modern methods that are 100 percent effective.

Postpartum Infecundability

The practices of breastfeeding and sexual abstinence after the birth of a child reduce a woman's exposure to becoming pregnant. Breastfeeding of long duration and on demand delays the return of a woman's normal pattern of ovulation. Cultural norms often prescribe limiting sexual relations after birth. In sub-Saharan Africa, both of these practices are utilized and are seen as necessary to protect the health of the child and the mother (van de Walle and van de Walle, 1988).

Tables 5-4 and 5-5 show the mean number of months of breastfeeding and postpartum amenorrhea, abstinence, and insusceptibility for currently married women by subgroup in Kenya at the times of the KFS and KDHS. In 1977-1978, the average duration of breastfeeding was 17.3 months, and the average duration of sexual abstinence was 3.9 months. In 1988-1989,

---

[2]Abstinence is excluded as a method (see the appendix to this chapter for justification).

TABLE 5-4   Mean Number of Months of Breastfeeding, Postpartum Amenorrhea, Postpartum Abstinence, and Postpartum Insusceptibility for Currently Married Women by Subgroup, 1977-1978 KFS

| Subgroup | Months | | | | Weighted No. of Births |
	Breastfeeding	Amenorrheic	Abstaining	Insusceptible[a]	
National	17.3	12.0	3.9	12.7	4,963
15-24	18.8	12.2	4.0	12.7	1,429
25-34	16.3	11.6	3.4	12.1	2,368
35-49	17.3	12.5	4.3	13.8	1,152
Residence					
Rural	17.6	12.3	3.8	12.9	4,426
Urban	14.7	10.0	4.2	10.5	537
Education					
None	18.7	13.6	4.6	14.2	2,361
1-4 years	16.7	12.1	3.7	12.8	1,016
5-7 years	16.2	9.8	2.8	10.4	1,183
8+ years	13.6	9.1	3.6	9.9	397
Province					
Nairobi	14.8	10.3	4.3	10.6	225
15-24	17.1	11.9	5.7	12.7	101
25-34	13.1	9.0	3.4	9.0	106
35-49	12.1	8.3	1.4	8.3	18
Central	14.5	10.5	2.7	11.0	749
15-24	16.5	9.4	2.7	10.1	154
25-34	13.5	10.6	2.4	10.9	367
35-49	14.7	11.1	3.0	11.9	228
Coast	18.1	13.8	3.2	14.0	383
15-24	21.9	14.0	3.7	14.0	129
25-34	16.4	11.7	2.7	12.2	180
35-49	15.8	18.5	3.5	18.7	74
Eastern	18.5	12.0	4.3	12.9	766
15-24	18.6	10.9	3.4	11.8	152
25-34	17.3	11.4	3.5	12.1	376
35-49	20.4	12.9	5.3	14.3	238
Nyanza	17.7	12.3	2.9	12.9	1,125
15-24	18.6	13.4	3.1	13.6	357
25-34	17.5	11.9	2.6	12.2	490
35-49	17.2	11.8	3.2	13.3	274
Rift Valley	17.6	13.1	6.6	14.0	988
15-24	19.7	13.8	6.4	14.2	300
25-34	16.8	12.4	6.0	13.3	486
35-49	16.5	13.8	8.4	15.9	193
Western	17.9	11.3	2.8	11.8	702
15-24	18.3	10.2	3.2	10.6	231
25-34	16.9	12.2	2.6	12.5	345
35-49	19.3	10.7	1.6	11.6	125

[a]Estimated as the mean number of months of postpartum amenorrhea or abstinence, whichever is longer.

TABLE 5-5   Mean Number of Months of Breastfeeding, Postpartum
Amenorrhea, Postpartum Abstinence, and Postpartum Insusceptibility for
Currently Married Women by Subgroup, 1988-1989 KDHS

Subgroup	Months Breastfeeding	Amenorrheic	Abstaining	Insusceptible[a]	Weighted No. of Births
National	20.1	11.2	3.9	11.7	3,667
15-24	20.9	11.4	4.5	11.9	1,016
25-34	19.5	10.7	3.4	11.1	1,787
35-49	20.3	11.8	4.4	12.6	864
Residence					
Rural	20.0	11.4	4.0	11.9	3,174
Urban	20.3	9.7	3.4	10.1	493
Education					
None	21.0	13.3	5.7	14.2	1,046
1-4 years	19.8	12.0	4.1	12.4	598
5-7 years	19.5	10.2	2.9	10.5	1,314
8+ years	20.0	9.3	3.2	9.6	705
Province and District					
Nairobi	21.7	9.7	4.2	10.3	208
15-24	22.3	10.7	4.5	11.6	98
25-34	20.9	8.8	3.8	9.1	92
35-49	23.1	9.0	5.2	9.0	18
Central	19.2	11.1	4.2	11.6	464
15-24	21.2	11.8	6.2	12.0	119
25-34	19.0	10.8	3.4	11.2	231
35-49	17.5	10.9	4.0	12.0	114
Kirinyaga	19.3	8.9	5.3	10.9	54
Muranga	21.7	11.4	3.0	11.9	108
Nyeri	16.5	9.0	3.9	9.6	141
Coast	19.1	10.0	2.1	10.1	223
15-24	17.0	10.7	3.0	10.9	59
25-34	20.7	9.8	2.3	9.8	112
35-49	18.2	9.9	0.7	9.9	52
Kilifi	19.5	9.9	1.7	10.1	88
Mombasa	17.8	9.7	3.8	9.7	55
Eastern	21.7	9.6	4.3	10.2	594
15-24	24.4	11.4	5.2	11.8	114
25-34	20.2	8.8	3.1	9.0	286
35-49	22.4	9.8	5.5	11.2	195
Machakos	24.0	10.6	3.5	11.2	261
Meru	21.6	10.0	4.9	10.5	146
Nyanza	19.3	11.5	2.2	11.9	677
15-24	19.7	10.8	2.1	11.3	207
25-34	18.3	11.3	2.1	11.7	322
35-49	20.8	12.8	2.5	13.2	149
Kisii	17.5	11.8	3.2	12.8	181

TABLE 5-5   *Continued*

| Subgroup | Months | | | | Weighted No. of Births |
	Breastfeeding	Amenorrheic	Abstaining	Insusceptible[a]	
Nyanza—*continued*					
Kisumu	21.0	9.1	2.8	9.3	208
Siaya	19.7	13.2	1.6	13.5	94
South Nyanza	19.0	12.9	0.8	13.1	193
Rift Valley	19.5	12.1	6.3	12.9	850
15-24	20.0	12.8	7.4	13.3	235
25-34	19.4	11.1	6.1	12.0	411
35-49	19.1	13.2	5.2	14.1	203
Kericho	20.6	11.2	4.9	12.3	179
Nakuru	17.1	10.4	3.3	10.4	113
Uasin Gishu	20.2	10.8	4.4	11.1	64
Western	20.4	12.1	2.8	12.3	651
15-24	21.2	10.8	2.3	11.2	184
25-34	19.5	12.2	2.1	12.2	333
35-49	21.6	13.6	5.0	14.0	134
Bungoma	20.3	11.4	2.1	11.5	183
Kakamega	19.3	10.8	2.6	11.0	361

[a]Estimated as the mean number of months of postpartum amenorrhea or abstinence, whichever is longer.

breastfeeding had increased to 20.1 months, which is surprising given that many populations experience reductions in length of breastfeeding as they develop economically. Because amenorrhea, which is determined by the length of breastfeeding, decreased by almost 1 month over the same period, this increase in breastfeeding may be more an artifact of the data than a reflection of what actually occurred.[3] The length of sexual abstinence did not change over time. By 1988-1989, the length of breastfeeding was approximately the same by type of residence and did not vary substantially across educational group. Length of amenorrhea and abstinence was longer in rural areas and among the least educated women.

The effect of postpartum amenorrhea and abstinence on fertility is measured by C_i, the index of postpartum infecundability.[4] When there is no

---

[3]The working group is not aware of any studies assessing the validity of this increase in breastfeeding or linking it to possible causal factors, such as breastfeeding campaigns or the price of food for children.

[4]Because C_i is calculated from the mean length of postpartum amenorrhea or abstinence, whichever is longer (see Appendix 5-1), the possible errors in the reported length of breastfeeding do not directly affect the estimate of C_i. However, if the increase in breastfeeding is real and is not reflected in an increase in the length of amenorrhea (due to misreporting), C_i will be overestimated.

lactation or postpartum abstinence, C_i equals 1; when infecundability is permanent, C_i equals 0.

Pathological or Primary Sterility

Primary sterility, or the inability of a woman to bear a child for biological reasons, has historically been high in sub-Saharan Africa, particularly in Central Africa (Frank, 1983; Bongaarts et al., 1984; Farley and Besley, 1988). In societies that value large families, such levels of sterility prevent some women who would like to bear children from doing so and lower the average level of fertility.

In this analysis, primary sterility is measured by the percentage of ever-married women age 40 to 49 who are childless. Table 5-6 gives the percentages for the KFS and KDHS. In 1977-1978, 3.1 percent of women were childless. Bongaarts et al. (1984) estimated that the standard rate of childlessness in developing countries is about 3 percent, indicating that Kenya was close to the standard and little excess sterility existed. However, there were substantial differentials among subgroups of the population. Urban areas demonstrated a very high level of primary sterility, with 9.7 percent childless. Primary sterility was higher among those women with no education than among those with some education. Nairobi and Coast provinces demonstrated fairly high levels of sterility, 8.2 and 7.2 percent, respectively.

TABLE 5-6   Women Aged 40-49 Who Are Childless by Subgroup, 1977-1978 and 1988-1989 (percent)

Subgroup	1977-1978	1988-1989
National	3.1	2.4
Residence		
Rural	2.7	2.1
Urban	9.7	5.6
Education		
None	3.8	2.9
1-4 years	1.5	1.9
5-7 years	0.0	0.5
8+ years	2.9	3.1
Province		
Nairobi	8.2	4.4
Central	1.3	1.9
Coast	7.2	2.1
Eastern	2.1	3.8
Nyanza	4.3	2.6
Rift	1.6	1.7
Western	3.3	1.5

By 1988-1989, the national level of primary sterility decreased to 2.4 percent. Sterility remained higher among urban women than rural women and among those women with no education than women with 1 to 7 years of education. Primary sterility was still highest in Nairobi; however, levels dropped dramatically to 2.1 percent in the Coast Province. Levels rose in Eastern by 1.7 percentage points to 3.8 percent.

Primary sterility is measured by the I_p index. Its calculation is based on a 3 percent standard rate of childlessness. When the rate of childlessness exceeds 3 percent, I_p is less than 1, indicating that fertility is inhibited. If the rate of childlessness is less than 3 percent, I_p is greater than 1, indicating that primary sterility is lower than expected in a developing country. Because levels of primary sterility in Kenya are often close to 3 percent, the index has little explanatory value in this analysis. Accordingly, the index is omitted from many of the figures; however, it is retained in the tables.

Furthermore, it is worth emphasizing that the numbers used to estimate primary sterility were calculated from very small samples. Therefore, the reliability of the numbers, particularly for subgroups of the population, is questionable.[5] The dramatic drop in sterility for Coast Province may reflect errors due to such small samples.

Abortion

There are very few data on abortion in Kenya, partly because the procedure is illegal except when a woman's life is in danger (Lema, 1990). However, some hospital data are available. In a study by Rogo (1990), it was noted that Kenyatta National Hospital in Nairobi treated 2,000 to 3,000 women for abortion complications in the late 1970s and early 1980s, and about 30 to 60 women a day, or 10,000 women a year, in 1990 (Jacobson, 1990). Lema et al. (1989) noted that 1,100 women were treated for abortion and its complications in eight district hospitals over 6 months. Case histories of primarily low-income urban women gathered in a study by Baker and Khasiani (1992) implied that abortion is fairly common, particularly among single and unemployed women.

Robinson and Harbison (1993) used the data from Kenyatta National Hospital in 1990 and the district hospitals to estimate an abortion rate of 25 procedures per 1,000 women per year, assuming that for every woman admitted to a hospital for abortion complications, four other women attempted an abortion. In this analysis, we use this estimate for C_a, the index of abortion. Unfortunately, not enough data were available to attempt to esti-

---

[5]Because of the unreliability of these estimates due to very small sample sizes, we have not calculated I_p for individual districts. We have used the province-level I_p as a proxy for each district.

mate an abortion rate for subgroups of the population; therefore, the national-level estimate is used for all subgroups as a very rough approximation of the effect of abortion on fertility, and the index is often omitted from the tables.

RESULTS

Tables 5-7 and 5-8 present the results of the proximate determinants analysis for the KFS and the KDHS. Figures 5-1 to 5-3 summarize the effects of marriage patterns, contraception, and postpartum infecundability on fertility for subgroups of the population.[6] The results are described below in detail.

Marriage

The effect of marriage patterns on fertility is summarized in the index C_m. In 1977-1978, C_m was .91; in 1988-1989, C_m was .86 (the lower the index, the stronger is the fertility-inhibiting effect). Marriage patterns reduced fertility by about 0.9 birth at the time of the KFS and by about 1.1 births at the time of the KDHS (i.e., if marriage were universal for all women of reproductive age, the average observed total fertility rate would increase, ceteris paribus, by 1.1 births in 1988-1989).[7] This strengthening of the fertility-inhibiting effect of marriage was due primarily to the increase in age at first union, described above. However, the change in C_m is not substantial or significant (reducing TF by only 0.2 birth), and it is important to note that significant childbearing occurs outside of union in Kenya, a fact that is not taken into account in calculating the C_m index. In fact, it has been estimated that age at first birth is lower than age at first marriage (Westoff, 1991a).

A similar pattern occurs across most of the subgroups: Changing marriage patterns have resulted in slightly lower fertility. Among the three age

---

[6]The results in the figures are presented using a logarithmic scale; thus, fertility reductions due to postpartum infecundability, contraceptive use, and nuptiality appear small because they are compressed.

[7]To express the effects of each index in births per woman, the following calculations are used (Bongaarts, 1982):

- The effect of marriage patterns equals TMFR − TFR, where TMFR equals TFR/C_m.
- The effect of contraception equals TNMF − TMFR, where TNMF equals $TFR/(C_m \cdot C_c)$.
- The effect of postpartum infecundability equals $(TFR/(C_m \cdot C_c \cdot C_i)) - TNMF$.

Care should be taken in interpreting these effects, expressed in births per woman, because the results depend on the order in which the effects are calculated. However, because Bongaarts et al. (1984) used this approach in their analysis of the proximate determinants of sub-Saharan Africa, we have done the same for consistency.

groups (15-24, early; 25-34, middle; and 35-49, late), marriage patterns had their greatest effect in the early age group, reflecting greater proportions of women single than in the other age groups. Because of later entry into union for urban and well-educated women, C_m had the strongest effect in inhibiting fertility among these two groups. The urban-rural differential is not as pronounced in the KDHS as in the KFS, which suggests that marriage patterns are becoming more similar for women across types of residence. Differentials have also narrowed among educational groups.

In comparing C_m across provinces for the 1988-1989 data, marriage patterns had their greatest effect in Central Province (C_m = .79), followed by Nairobi (C_m = .83). They had their weakest effect in Eastern, Nyanza, and Western provinces. In 1977-1978, marriage patterns inhibited fertility most substantially in Nairobi, Eastern, and Central, in that order. At the district level, in 1988-1989, Kirinyaga and Meru had the lowest C_m (.79 for both).

Contraception

The dramatic increase in contraceptive use between 1977-1978 and 1988-1989 is reflected in a decrease in C_c from .95 to .76, or a reduction in fertility of about two births. The greater fertility-inhibiting effect of C_c is reflected across all subgroups. Although there was little variation in the effect of contraception among the three age groups in 1977-1978, differentials increased by 1989, when contraceptive use had its greatest effect on fertility among the middle and late age groups.[8] These differentials indicate higher contraceptive prevalence, as well as use of more effective methods, among women 25 years and older.

As expected, contraception inhibits fertility most among urban and well-educated women. Although differentials did not change by type of residence between the two surveys, there was greater variation in C_c among educational groups in 1988-1989.

In 1988-1989 among the provinces, contraception had its greatest fertility-inhibiting effect in Central, Eastern, and Nairobi in that order, reflecting the highest contraceptive prevalence rates. These same three provinces had the lowest C_c in 1977-1978, but only Nairobi exhibited a very strong index (.85 versus indices greater than .92 for the other two). In 1988-1989,

---

[8]It should be noted that the formula for C_c (see the appendix at end of chapter for the exact calculation) has not been modified for each age group. At issue is the 1.08 value that adjusts for the proportion of women who are fecund, which varies with age. The 1.08 value is a weighted average of age-specific indicators and is meant to apply to women 15-49. The 1.08 value has been used for each age group separately because more refined age-specific values would not give significantly different results than those generated in this analysis.

TABLE 5-7 Proximate Determinants by Subgroup, 1977-1978

Subgroup	Observed TFR	Index of Marriage, C_m	Index of Contraception, C_c	Index of Postpartum Infecundability, C_i	Index of Sterility, I_p	Index of Abortion, C_a	Model Estimate of Total Fecundity Rate, TF
National	8.15	.91	.95	.64	1.00	.92	16.1
15-24	2.61	.81	.97	.64	1.00	.92	5.6
25-34	3.22	.97	.94	.65	1.00	.92	5.9
35-49	2.32	.95	.95	.62	1.00	.92	4.6
Residence							
Rural	8.36	.92	.96	.64	1.00	.92	16.2
Urban	6.07	.84	.89	.69	.90	.92	14.1
Education							
None	8.15	.96	.97	.61	.99	.92	15.8
1-4 years	8.97	.93	.95	.64	1.02	.92	16.9
5-7 years	7.91	.90	.93	.69	1.05	.92	14.2
8+ years	6.95	.83	.83	.70	1.00	.92	15.7
Province							
Nairobi	5.79	.82	.85	.69	.92	.92	14.2
15-24	2.16	.72	.93	.64	.92	.92	6.0
25-34	2.77	.90	.76	.73	.92	.92	6.5
35-49	.86	.88	.84	.75	.92	.92	1.9
Central	8.54	.88	.92	.68	1.03	.92	16.6
15-24	2.37	.74	.93	.70	1.03	.92	5.2
25-34	3.44	.98	.92	.68	1.03	.92	6.0
35-49	2.73	.90	.92	.66	1.03	.92	5.3

Coast	6.96	.96	.96	.62	.94	.92	14.2
15-24	2.55	.89	.97	.62	.94	.92	5.6
25-34	2.69	1.02	.95	.65	.94	.92	4.9
35-49	1.72	.99	.96	.54	.94	.92	3.9
Eastern	8.22	.86	.94	.64	1.01	.92	17.2
15-24	2.35	.70	.94	.66	1.01	.92	5.8
25-34	3.24	.96	.93	.65	1.01	.92	5.9
35-39	2.63	.92	.94	.61	1.01	.92	5.4
Nyanza	8.14	.95	.97	.64	.98	.92	15.4
15-24	2.77	.87	.99	.62	.98	.92	5.8
25-34	3.13	.99	.96	.65	.98	.92	5.6
35-49	2.24	1.01	.97	.63	.98	.92	4.0
Rift Valley	8.78	.91	.95	.62	1.02	.92	17.6
15-24	2.89	.85	.97	.61	1.02	.92	6.1
25-34	3.35	.97	.94	.63	1.02	.92	6.2
35-49	2.54	.90	.94	.58	1.02	.92	5.5
Western	8.02	.93	.97	.66	1.00	.92	14.7
15-24	2.78	.85	.97	.69	1.00	.92	5.3
25-34	3.39	.97	.99	.65	1.00	.92	6.0
35-49	1.85	.97	.95	.66	1.00	.92	3.3

TABLE 5-8 Proximate Determinants by Subgroup, 1988-1989

Subgroup	Observed TFR	Index of Marriage, C_m	Index of Contraception, C_c	Index of Postpartum Infecundability, C_i	Index of Sterility, I_p	Index of Abortion, C_a	Model Estimate of Total Fecundity Rate, TF
National	6.62	.86	.76	.66	1.01	.92	16.5
15-24	2.34	.75	.84	.66	1.01	.92	6.1
25-34	2.70	.94	.75	.68	1.01	.92	6.1
35-49	1.58	.92	.72	.64	1.01	.92	4.0
Residence							
Rural	6.98	.87	.77	.66	1.01	.92	17.0
Urban	4.71	.82	.71	.70	.96	.92	13.1
Education							
None	7.23	.91	.84	.61	1.00	.92	16.8
1-4 years	7.65	.94	.77	.65	1.02	.92	17.4
5-7 years	7.15	.88	.74	.69	1.04	.92	16.7
8+ years	4.95	.82	.65	.71	1.00	.92	14.2
Province and District							
Nairobi	4.48	.83	.68	.69	.98	.92	12.6
15-24	1.87	.73	.82	.66	.98	.92	5.2
25-34	1.77	.84	.64	.72	.98	.92	5.1
35-49	.84	1.17	.53	.73	.98	.92	2.1
Central	5.83	.79	.63	.66	1.02	.92	18.7
15-24	1.92	.61	.74	.66	1.02	.92	7.0
25-34	2.53	.95	.64	.67	1.02	.92	6.6
35-49	1.38	.91	.58	.66	1.02	.92	4.3
Kirinyaga	5.21	.79	.52	.68	1.02	.92	20.2
Muranga	6.12	.87	.68	.66	1.02	.92	16.8
Nyeri	6.47	.80	.61	.71	1.02	.92	19.9

Coast	5.25	.85	.84	.70	1.01	.92	11.3
15-24	2.01	.81	.94	.68	1.01	.92	4.1
25-34	2.03	.89	.78	.71	1.01	.92	4.4
35-49	1.21	.86	.83	.70	1.01	.92	2.6
Kilifi	6.55	.92	.90	.70	1.01	.92	12.1
Mombasa	4.48	.93	.77	.71	1.01	.92	9.5
Eastern	6.91	.90	.66	.70	.99	.92	18.4
15-24	2.26	.83	.74	.66	.99	.92	6.2
25-34	2.95	.96	.63	.73	.99	.92	7.4
35-39	1.70	.90	.65	.67	.99	.92	4.8
Machakos	7.67	.93	.67	.67	.99	.92	20.3
Meru	6.13	.79	.56	.69	.99	.92	18.7
Nyanza	7.11	.90	.38	.66	1.01	.92	14.8
15-24	2.67	.82	.92	.67	1.01	.92	5.7
25-34	2.83	.97	.88	.66	1.01	.92	5.4
35-49	1.61	.93	.85	.63	1.01	.92	3.5
Kisii	7.13	.86	.81	.64	1.01	.92	17.4
Kisumu	7.87	.88	.83	.72	1.01	.92	16.0
Siaya	6.53	.90	.93	.63	1.01	.92	13.5
South Nyanza	6.98	1.01	.95	.63	1.01	.92	12.5
Rift Valley	7.03	.86	.74	.64	1.02	.92	18.5
15-24	2.56	.73	.78	.63	1.02	.92	7.6
25-34	2.65	.93	.74	.66	1.02	.92	6.2
35-49	1.82	.97	.72	.61	1.02	.92	4.5
Kericho	8.03	.90	.80	.65	1.02	.92	18.4
Nakuru	6.92	.88	.58	.69	1.02	.92	20.8
Uasin Gishu	6.36	.89	.89	.68	1.02	.92	12.7
Western	7.76	.90	.88	.65	1.02	.92	16.2
15-24	2.72	.80	.95	.67	1.02	.92	5.6
25-34	3.41	.98	.86	.65	1.02	.92	6.6
35-49	1.63	.91	.84	.62	1.02	.92	3.7
Bungoma	8.27	.93	.92	.67	1.02	.92	15.5
Kakamega	7.46	.90	.87	.68	1.02	.92	15.0

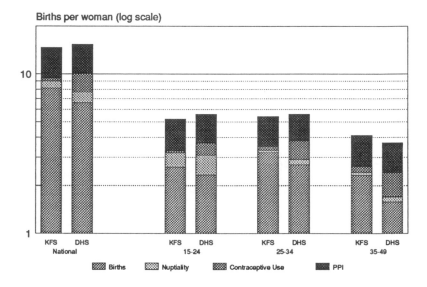

FIGURE 5-1   Proximate determinants, national and by age group, KFS and KDHS.
NOTE: PPI, Postpartum infecundability.

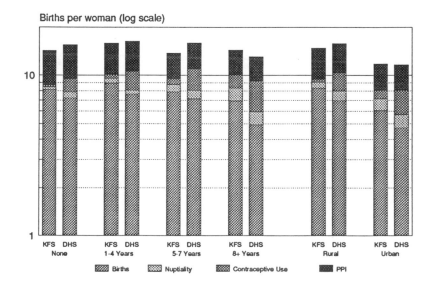

FIGURE 5-2   Proximate determinants by education and residence, KFS and KDHS.
NOTE: PPI, Postpartum infecundability.

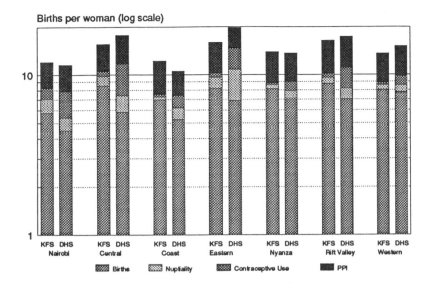

FIGURE 5-3 Proximate determinants by province, KFS and KDHS. NOTE: PPI, Postpartum infecundability.

among the districts, Kirinyaga had an exceptionally low C_c (.52), followed by Nakuru (.58). South Nyanza, Siaya, Bungoma, and Kilifi showed relatively weak contraceptive use effects.

Postpartum Infecundability

The index of postpartum infecundability C_i had the greatest effect of all the indices at the national level. C_i remained relatively unchanged between the two surveys (.64 for KFS and .66 for KDHS) and reduced fertility by more than five births. Furthermore, little change in C_i is evident across subgroups, except for a weakening (increase in C_i) in Coast and Eastern provinces. Because of longer periods of postpartum amenorrhea and abstinence among rural and little-educated women, C_i had its greatest fertility-inhibiting effect in these two groups at both times. Its effect consistently weakens with increased education.

At both times, Western and Rift Valley provinces had the lowest C_i. Siaya, South Nyanza, and Kisii, all in Nyanza Province, had the longest nonsusceptible period of the districts, which is reflected in very low C_i.

Primary Sterility

Primary sterility generally had little effect on fertility across subgroups in Kenya from 1977-1978 to 1988-1989. However, it did have an effect on the fertility of urban women, particularly in the KFS. Nairobi and Coast showed an effect in 1977-1978, but this effect was eliminated by 1988-1989, reflecting either a drop in rates of primary sterility due to improved medical care or sample sizes that were too small to yield reliable estimates.

Summary

In looking at the national-level indices from the 1988-1989 KDHS, the most important fertility-suppressing index is postpartum infecundability, followed by contraception, and then marriage. Abortion and primary sterility had limited effects. Results from the 1977-1978 KFS also indicate that postpartum infecundability was the most important fertility-inhibiting variable at the national level. Marriage patterns (C_m) followed in significance in the earlier period, with contraception having a relatively minor effect. What is most notable is the substantial change between the two surveys in contraceptive use patterns, which replaced marriage as the second most important fertility-inhibiting factor at the later date. This decline in C_c is due to increasing contraceptive prevalence, since the method use-effectiveness mix has changed very little. C_m also declined between the two surveys, although not as steeply as C_c. The effects of infecundability and primary sterility (C_i and I_p) changed little.

The indices by subgroup generally follow the national pattern, with postpartum infecundability as the most important fertility-suppressing variable, followed by contraception and marriage for the KDHS and by marriage and contraception for the KFS. There are a few notable exceptions. For all of the seven provinces included in the surveys, postpartum infecundability had the greatest fertility-suppressing effect of the proximate determinants in 1977-1978. In 1988-1989, it had the largest effect for only four of the seven provinces: Coast, Nyanza, Rift Valley, and Western. For the other provinces—Nairobi, Central, and Eastern—contraceptive practices had the greatest impact on fertility. However, for all the provinces, the effect of contraception in inhibiting fertility increased over time, due to substantial increases in contraceptive use, as shown in Figure 5-4. Among educational groups, contraceptive practices surpassed postpartum infecundability in suppressing fertility only in the most-educated group. However, contraceptive use increased dramatically for all subgroups between the two surveys, as shown in Figure 5-5.

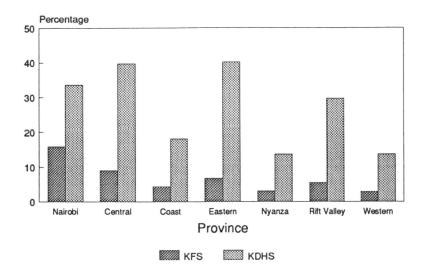

FIGURE 5-4   Current contraceptive use by province for women in union—KFS and KDHS.

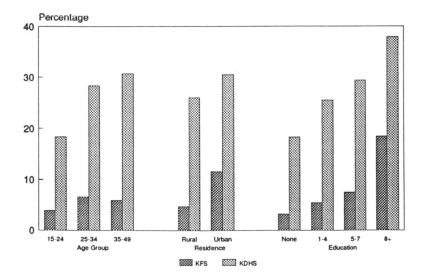

FIGURE 5-5   Current contraceptive use by subgroup for women in union—KFS and KDHS.

RELATION BETWEEN CHANGES IN
PROXIMATE DETERMINANTS AND FERTILITY

The proximate determinant indices of the Bongaarts framework have been estimated from the KFS and KDHS data by identical methods. They can be taken as applicable to the few years preceding the surveys, although the exact time specification varies from index to index. For practical purposes, the changes between the two surveys can be set against the corresponding changes in fertility as measured by the total fertility rates calculated for the previous 5 years. KFS and KDHS fertility estimates are available by provinces, by urban and rural residence, and by the education of the mother. The KFS sample sizes by districts were too small for usable indices of proximate determinants to be derived.

Table 5-9 shows levels based on data from the KDHS as a percentage of the KFS values. The index C_a was omitted because it was taken as constant throughout and makes no contribution to the calculation of change. The estimated total fertilities in the 5 years before the KDHS as a percentage of the corresponding measures from the KFS are presented in parallel. By using the Bongaarts model, if the estimates are reliable, the change in the product $(I_p \cdot C_m \cdot C_c \cdot C_i \cdot C_a)$ should equal the change in the total fertility. For Kenya as a whole, the agreement is excellent, with a 21 percent reduction in the proximate determinants effect compared to the 19 percent decline in fertility. For the subpopulations, such good correspondence is not

TABLE 5-9 Proximate Determinant and Fertility Indices from the KDHS as Percentages of KFS Measures

Subgroup	I_p	C_m	C_c	C_i	Product	TFR
National	101	95	80	103	79	81
Provinces						
Nairobi	107	101	80	100	86	74
Central	99	90	68	97	59	69
Coast	107	89	87	113	94	73
Eastern	98	105	70	109	79	84
Nyanza	103	95	91	103	92	87
Rift Valley	100	94	78	103	76	80
Western	102	97	91	98	88	96
Urban/Rural						
Urban	107	98	80	101	85	77
Rural	101	95	80	103	79	83
Education						
No schooling	101	95	87	100	84	86
1-4 years	100	101	81	101	83	85
5+ years	99	98	79	100	77	83

to be expected. Sample errors could be quite substantial with the comparatively small numbers, particularly for the component indices I_p and C_m. In allowing for this possibility, the agreement for the education subgroups is satisfactory, which confirms the small variation in fertility decline by education. The changes in urban and rural proximate determinants indicate a reversal from the reductions in total fertility rates, that is, a greater decline in rural areas. The discrepancy is not large, however, and seems to arise from the I_p measure, which is particularly vulnerable.

For the provinces, given the sample errors, the correspondence between changes in fertility and the proximate determinants product is reasonable for Central, Nyanza, Rift Valley, and Eastern. The problems of estimating valid measures for Nairobi have been noted in the chapter on fertility. The implication of the determinants for Western is that the estimated fertility decline of 4 percent is too small; the earlier breakdown of this decline by age of women had also raised doubts about reliability. The major discrepancy, however, is for the Coast, where a 27 percent decline in fertility is associated with only a 6 percent decline in the combined proximate determinants. The small overall decline arises from substantial reductions in C_m and C_c, offset by large rises in I_p and C_i. The latter are puzzling. At the time of the KFS, the Coast had the lowest I_p index of all the provinces except Nairobi (i.e., the highest reported childlessness among ever-married women aged 40-49 years) and the lowest C_i value (the longest insusceptible period following a birth). At the time of the KDHS the ranking of the Coast was largely reversed, with little childlessness reported by 40- to 49-year-old ever-married women and the shortest insusceptible period among the provinces (4 months less than that obtained from the KFS). The national changes in these measures between the two surveys were small. Such an extreme alteration in these biosocial parameters for the Coast is very implausible, and data errors must be suspected. If the I_p and C_i changes for the Coast are ignored and only the product $C_m \cdot C_c$ is considered, the KDHS value is 77 percent of the KFS level, which implies a fertility decline of 23 percent in rather good agreement with the directly estimated 27 percent. The use of the $C_m \cdot C_c$ product only to assess the effects of changes in the proximate determinants gives, on average, slightly better agreement for the other provinces also.

Apart from the measures for the Coast, which are of doubtful validity, the I_p and C_i indices showed little change between the KFS and KDHS for the individual provinces. The movements in C_m were also rather small, except possibly in Central and Coast provinces. It can be noted that the large decline in the fertility of young women in the Coast also suggests an effect of later marriage.

The reductions in the proximate determinant product from the KFS to the KDHS are thus, in general, dominated by the increase in contraceptive use as gauged by the C_c index. The reduction in this index is reflected almost exactly in the total fertility rate decline for Kenya as a whole, very closely for Central and Rift Valley provinces, and with reasonable agreement for Nairobi and Nyanza. The Coast comparison suggests that in this region, later marriage may also have made a substantial contribution to the fertility decline. The comparison for Eastern Province is less convincing because the increase in contraceptive use would have been expected to produce a greater fertility decline than that recorded.

A similar examination at the district level is precluded by the small sample sizes of the KFS. An attempt at a rough assessment is presented in Table 5-10. It has been assumed in the calculations that the proximate determinant indices for districts at the KFS can be taken to be the same as for the provinces that contain them at the same time. The crudeness of this assumption is obvious. It may be satisfactory for the more homogeneous provinces such as Central and Western but is highly suspect for the diverse Rift Valley. However, the C_c indices at the KFS were all rather close to 1 because of low contraceptive use in all provinces except Nairobi (.85) and Central (.92). The scope for error due to the assumption is thus small here.

There is a broad association between the percentage reductions in fertil-

TABLE 5-10 Reductions in Fertility and Proximate Determinants, KFS to KDHS (percent)

District	Cumulated Fertility[a]	Product $C_m \cdot C_c \cdot C_i \cdot I_p$	C_c
Kirinyaga	36	50	43
Siaya	27	8	4
Uasin Gishu	26	0	6
Nyeri	24	38	34
Nakuru	23	35	39
Kericho	22	13	16
Meru	22	32	30
Muranga	21	30	26
Mombasa	20	4	20
Kilifi	19	−9	6
Kisii	19	22	16
Machakos	12	21	29
Kakamega	10	9	10
Bungoma	8	2	5
Kisumu	7	8	14
South Nyanza	7	−6	2

NOTE: Proximate determinants indices for the districts at the KFS are taken to be the same as for the provinces that contain them.

[a]From KDHS, 1974-1978 to 1984-1988, women under 40 years.

ity and in the proximate determinants. Thus, Kirinyaga, Nyeri, and Nakuru had the largest reductions in C_c and the combined product: They are near the top of the ranking for fertility declines. The districts with the four smallest fertility declines (Kakamega, Bungoma, Kisumu, and South Nyanza) showed only modest changes in the proximate determinants. But there are striking inconsistencies, notably for Siaya and Uasin Gishu, which recorded the second and third highest fertility declines but negligible alterations in C_c and the product index. The doubts about the fertility measure for Siaya are discussed in Chapter 4. Plots of the fertility declines against the changes in proximate determinants are shown in Figures 5-6A (combined product) and 5-6B (C_c index). The latter relation is closer, particularly if the regression line is constrained to pass through the origin. To a large extent, the closer relation is due to the improved agreement for Kilifi and Mombasa in the Coast Province, where the I_p and C_i changes are suspect. As has been pointed out, this examination is subject to considerable uncertainty because of data limitations and errors, chance fluctuations due to small numbers, and crudeness of assumptions. Despite these caveats, the general agreement of the estimates of fertility decline with the changes in proximate determinants gives strong support to the belief that the findings of our analysis of the proximate determinants are broadly reliable.

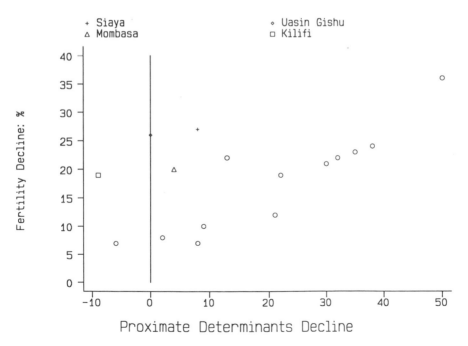

FIGURE 5-6A   Declines in fertility and proximate determinant indices.

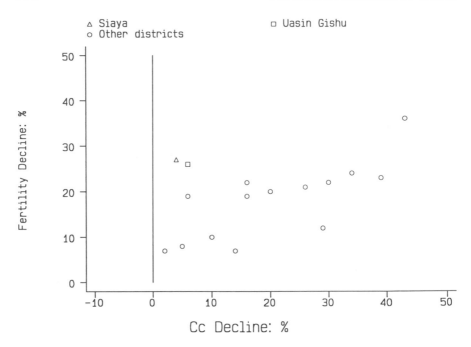

FIGURE 5-6B   Declines in fertility and C_c (index of contraception).

COMPARISONS OF THE PROXIMATE DETERMINANTS OF KENYA WITH OTHER SUB-SAHARAN POPULATIONS

Table 5-11 gives the indices for the proximate determinants at the aggregate level for all the populations in sub-Saharan Africa for which a DHS had been conducted and a standard recode data tape made available as of 1992. The results for Botswana and Zimbabwe, two countries that have also experienced a notable drop in fertility, show that contraception was an important inhibitor of fertility at the time of the surveys, in contrast to the findings for the other sub-Saharan African populations shown.[9]   Sudan, which may also have experienced a fertility decline (Sudan Department of Statistics and Institute for Resource Development, 1991), showed a fairly weak C_c, but an exceptionally strong effect of marriage patterns (see Jolly and Gribble, 1993, for a fuller discussion).

Like Kenya in 1977-1978, most of sub-Saharan African fertility at the time of the DHS was inhibited primarily by postpartum infecundability, followed in most cases by marriage patterns. The question remains whether these countries will follow the pattern of Botswana, Kenya, and Zimbabwe of increased contraceptive use and lower fertility.

---

[9]Unfortunately, data from the nationally representative survey of Nigeria were not available at the time this table was constructed.

TABLE 5-11 Proximate Determinants of Fertility, Other DHS Sample Populations in Sub-Saharan Africa

Country	Observed TFR	Index of Marriage, C_m	Index of Contraception, C_c	Index of Postpartum Infecundability, C_i	Index of Sterility, I_p	Model Estimate of Total Fecundity Rate, TF
Botswana 1988	4.97	.873	.692	.629	.998	13.1
Burundi 1987	6.92	.801	.948	.525	1.029	16.9
Ghana 1988	6.35	.850	.894	.552	1.021	14.8
Kenya 1988-1989	6.62	.860	.761	.662	1.009	15.1
Liberia 1986	6.69	.932	.939	.588	1.000	13.0
Mali 1987	7.04	.976	.973	.563	.994	13.2
Ondo State, Nigeria 1986-1987	6.09	.826	.949	.472	1.033	15.9
Senegal 1986	6.57	.898	.959	.554	.976	14.1
Sudan 1989-1990	4.87	.680	.925	.599	.989	13.1
Togo 1988	6.59	.865	.905	.518	1.021	15.9
Uganda 1988-1989	7.35	.918	.958	.627	.967	13.8
Zimbabwe 1988-1989	5.49	.812	.597	.658	1.005	17.1

SOURCE: Jolly and Gribble (1993).

SUMMARY

Examination of the changes in the proximate determinants of fertility in Kenya from the late 1970s to the late 1980s reveals the primary importance of increasing contraceptive use in the fertility decline over this same period. Although postpartum infecundability continued to have the strongest fertility-inhibiting effect of all the proximate determinants, contraceptive use replaced marriage patterns as the second most important fertility-inhibiting factor. Comparing the changes in the proximate determinants with the declines in fertility shows almost equal reductions in both, indicating that the results of the analysis are generally credible.

APPENDIX

COMPUTATIONAL PROCEDURES TO ESTIMATE THE INDICES OF THE PROXIMATE DETERMINANTS

Marriage Patterns

$$C_m = \frac{\text{total fertility rate (TFR)}}{\text{total marital fertility rate (TMFR)}}$$

where TFR = average total number of births a woman would have in her lifetime at current age-specific fertility rates (ASFRs), and TMFR = average total number of births a woman in union throughout her reproductive years would have in her lifetime at current age-specific marital fertility rates.

Both rates were estimated for the four years prior to the survey. The TMFR was estimated for women currently in union.

Contraception

$$C_c = 1 - 1.08ue,$$

where u = current contraceptive use prevalence rate among women in sexual union, and e = average use-effectiveness of contraception.

Abstinence is excluded as a method because it was listed as a potential response only on the KFS questionnaire and not on the DHS, and because many of the women who reported using abstinence as a contraceptive method were practicing postpartum abstinence, which is captured in the C_i index. Periodic abstinence or rhythm method, however, is included as a method.

The average use-effectiveness of a method is calculated as the weighted average of the method-specific use-effectiveness levels, with the weights equal to the proportion of women using a given method. The levels used were adapted by Bongaarts and Potter (1983) from a study by Laing (1978) in the Philippines. They are

Pill	0.90
IUD	0.95
Sterilization	1.00
Other methods	0.70

Postpartum Infecundability

$$C_i = 20/(18.5 + i),$$

where i = mean number of months of postpartum infecundability (estimated as mean number of months of postpartum amenorrhea or abstinence, whichever is longer) for women in union. The mean number of months of post-partum infecundability is estimated by using the prevalence/incidence method. In this analysis,

$$i = \frac{\text{number of mothers either amenorrheic or abstaining at time of survey (prevalence)}}{\text{average number of births per month over last 36 months (incidence)}}$$

Primary Sterility

$$I_p = (7.63 - .11s)/7.3,$$

where s = proportion of married women between ages 40 and 49 who have never had a child.

Bongaarts et al. (1984) used the percentage of women age 45-49 who were childless. In this analysis, the percentage of childless women age 40-49 is used to increase the number of women in each subgroup and reduce the standard error in estimating s. It is assumed that all women had their first child by age 40 in Kenya.

Abortion

$$C_a = \frac{\text{TFR}}{\text{TFR} + A},$$

where $A = 0.4(1 + u)\text{TA}$, u = contraceptive prevalence rate, and TA = number of abortions per female during her reproductive years.

Total Natural Fecundity Rate

$$\text{TF} = \text{TFR}/(C_m \cdot C_c \cdot C_i \cdot I_p \cdot C_a)$$

(Bongaarts and Potter, 1983; Bongaarts et al., 1984).

6

Socioeconomic and Program Factors
Related to Fertility Change

The analysis in Chapter 5 indicates the relative importance of several proximate determinants in the fertility decline that occurred in Kenya from the mid-1970s to the late 1980s. In this chapter we go beyond the proximate determinants to the underlying socioeconomic factors that, in turn, affect the increases in the age of marriage and the increase in the proportion using contraception. Our question is: What are the socioeconomic changes that have led to these behavioral changes on the part of women and men in Kenya? For many of these factors, it appears that the changes have been strongly affected by government policy and program initiatives. Thus, in this chapter we also look at the evolution and effects of these initiatives.

ANALYTICAL FRAMEWORK

In thinking about these changes it is helpful to have some analytical framework guiding our discussion. The essence of a fertility transition such as Kenya is experiencing is a movement from an uncontrolled natural fertility regime to a situation in which individuals plan their childbearing and attempt to reach some target family size using whatever means are at their disposal. The relatively constant total fertility rates of more than 8.0 during the 1960s and 1970s almost certainly indicate that natural fertility prevailed in Kenya at that time. As we have seen, this situation has changed dramatically in the last 10 to 15 years. There are now quite striking variations in fertility and also in the proximate determinants at the province and district level. Thus, it seems that natural fertility is giving way to planned fertility.

If we accept this, what socioeconomic factors are likely to be associated with decreasing desired or intended family size and, consequently, with growing efforts to control fertility? More particularly, which policies and programs launched by the government of Kenya had the greatest effect on these changed fertility goals and processes?

The most widely known theoretical framework found in the current literature suggests that couples do attempt to maximize over time the well-being of their immediate household/family group and that fertility plans are made in this context (Easterlin and Crimmins, 1985). That is, the expected benefits to the household or gains from children are balanced against perceived costs and disadvantages, and a target outcome results. Thus, socioeconomic factors affect fertility plans by affecting the perceptions of the benefits and costs of various family sizes. Government policies and programs also will have an effect on fertility through these channels. Fertility intentions become real fertility outcomes through the use of some technology to control fertility. The availability of modern contraceptives can also affect fertility outcomes by making couples more effective planners. Policy and program have effects, in this fashion, by introducing the means of contraception, or making them cheaper (Berelson, 1977).

Without accepting all the tenets of this economic model, it is helpful to organize our discussion around this framework of demand and supply of children. That is, we assume that certain socioeconomic policies and programs affect the perceived costs and benefits of children and hence the demand for them by couples. Other programs affect the cost of controlling fertility. The potential supply of children can also be affected by socioeconomic policies and programs, but these appear less significant in the present case.

In the next section, we discuss changes in reproductive preferences in Kenya, which serve as an indicator of the demand for children. We then outline the socioeconomic and program factors that are associated with changes in preferences and ability to meet them.

CHANGES IN REPRODUCTIVE PREFERENCES

The Kenya Fertility Survey (KFS), the Kenya Contraceptive Prevalence Survey (KCPS), and the Kenya Demographic and Health Survey (KDHS) collected data on ideal family size and preferences for bearing another child. These data serve as indicators of fertility norms and intentions and are useful in suggesting the demand for family planning.

As discussed in Chapter 2, reproductive preferences in Kenya have changed dramatically between 1977-1978 and 1988-1989. The proportion of currently married women who desire no more children increased from 17.0 to 50.9 percent, and the mean ideal family size among all women dropped from 6.2 to 4.4 children. Such large changes (in percentage terms)

TABLE 6-1 Percentage of Currently Married Fecund[a] Women Who Want No More Children By Age Group, KFS, KCPS, and KDHS

Age Group	Survey Date		
	1977-1978	1984	1988-1989
15-19	2	3.8	9.3
20-24	4	10.7	18.4
25-29	12	23.4	39.5
30-34	19	45.0	57.3
35-39	25	53.7	69.7
40-44	40	66.6	83.5
45-49	42	75.9	89.0
Total	17	31.5	50.9

[a]Women who state they are capable of having another child.

in fertility preferences have not been documented elsewhere in sub-Saharan Africa.

Table 6-1 shows the percentage of currently married women (by age group) who wanted no more children for all three surveys. The desire for no more children increased for all age groups from 1977-1978 to 1988-1989. For example, at the first period, only 25 percent of women aged 35-39 wanted no more children; in 1988-1989, 69.7 percent of women in this age group wanted no more children. The most recent data (KDHS) indicate that the percentage of women who wanted no more children is positively associated with the number of living children (data not shown). Although only 3 percent of women with one child wanted no more children, 82 percent of women with six or more children wanted no more children, indicating a strong desire to limit family size. There was also significant interest in spacing births. Approximately 50 percent of women with one or two children wanted to wait at least 2 years before their next birth.[1]

In summary, substantial changes in fertility preferences occurred over the 11-year period between the KFS and the KDHS. If women could have the ideal number of children they say they want, the total fertility rate in

---

[1]Westoff and Ochoa (1991) used these fertility preferences data to measure unmet need for family planning, as indicated by the proportion of women who are exposed to the risk of conception, are not using a contraceptive method, and say they want to delay or limit childbearing. They found that in 1988-1989, 38 percent of currently married women in Kenya were in need of family planning, with about 60 percent of these women wanting to delay their next birth and about 40 percent wanting to limit childbearing. The measures indicate greater unmet need in urban than in rural areas and among women with primary education than no education or at least secondary education. Overall, unmet need increased 129 percent between 1977-1978 and 1988-1989.

Kenya would drop by about two births (Westoff, 1991b). The discrepancy between actual and desired TFR indicates a strong demand for family planning as well as the likelihood that fertility will continue to decline.

GROWTH OF GOVERNMENT PROGRAMS

In Chapter 2, we allude briefly to the emphasis the government of Kenya has placed on improving the nation's physical infrastructure, and its education and health systems. Capital spending for these three objectives was heavy, particularly during the first decade of Kenya's independence. Recurrent expenditures for the latter two program areas have continued to be substantial (see Table 6-2). Currently, education and health alone account for nearly one-quarter of all government spending in Kenya. The development strategy followed by Kenya has emphasized the creation of social and capital infrastructure: human capital through education and health, and physical capital through roads, transport, communications, and other facilities. The linkages and economic spillovers generated from this infra-

TABLE 6-2   Central Government Expenditures in Kenya by Broad Categories (percent by fiscal years)

	1975	1980	1985	1990
Administration	15.0	17.3	12.7	15.6
Defense	6.3	14.6	7.8	5.2
Education	21.2	17.7	20.2	18.9
Health	6.9	7.1	5.7	4.9
Social security and welfare	0.0	2.2	3.9[a]	3.7[a]
Housing and community development	3.7	1.3		
Agriculture	11.3	7.8	14.3[b]	17.3[b]
Manufacturing and construction	2.2	1.9		
Electricity and water	2.9	4.4	6.9[c]	6.9[c]
Roads	8.7	6.5		
Communication	4.5	2.5		
Other	14.6	15.3	28.4[d]	27.1[d]
Transfers to other government agencies	2.6	1.4		
Total	99.9	100.0	100.0	100.0

[a]Includes housing and community development
[b]Includes manufacturing and construction.
[c]Includes roads and communication.
[d]Includes transfers to other government agencies.

SOURCES: World Bank (1983); Kenya (1991a).

structure for the mainly private productive sectors of the economy have no doubt contributed to the rapid rates of increase in the gross domestic product (World Bank, 1980 and 1983).

A fact well worth noting is that the high priority assigned to this social overhead investment, human and physical, was a Kenyan decision. Kenyan political leaders and their technicians believed that there was a deep-rooted, widespread demand throughout the country for health and education services; they also believed that improved internal communications and transportation were necessary to unite the country, and would also be popular with the masses. In retrospect, these appear to have been correct intuitions. But the donor groups, who were paying for a large share of the development budgets, frequently argued that Kenya was moving too fast and "overinvesting" in these areas. For example, a World Bank (1963:223) economic review commenting on educational issues stated, "Although the enthusiasm for education in Kenya and the striking advances that have been made are in many respects admirable, they will pose a major problem . . . the mission urges policies of restraint towards further enlargement of primary education in Kenya." The same report advised against a planned expansion of hospital facilities and said, "While there is an urgent need to meet particular deficiencies . . . we do not believe a general expansion of hospital and health facilities can be undertaken" (World Bank, 1963:309). The World Bank mission was equally skeptical about proposed road construction and, in particular, recommended against the reconstruction of the Nairobi-Mombasa highway. The report stated, "The mission considers that this work should be postponed until more essential projects have been undertaken, including those in other fields of development" (World Bank, 1963:333).

Ten years later, another World Bank report sounded similar cautious notes about the pace and direction of much of Kenya's development spending. It singled out road construction and telecommunications and warned that a "momentum" had been built up that would be difficult to slow down. It added, "A similar situation can be seen within the social services . . . no one can deny that education, health, and other services are justified on economic and humanitarian grounds . . . but the past rate of increase is such that some curb is essential if it is not to run away with the budget" (World Bank, 1975:37). Other donor reports reflected a similar concern that Kenya was overinvesting in human and capital infrastructure, and was neglecting agriculture and industry. But the programs went forward anyway and achieved remarkable gains.

Transportation and Communication

In the case of roads, there was an increase from 50,000 to 64,000 kilometers between 1975 and 1991, a 25 percent increase. Given the fact that many of the existing roads were improved and upgraded as well, the overall expansion in the efficiency and usability of the system was even greater than these figures would indicate. More than one-third of this increase was in the Rift Valley Province. At the district level, Machakos in Eastern Province was the greatest beneficiary. The number of licensed public passenger service vehicles (buses, minivans, etc.) and freight transport vehicles increased by 50 percent, from 8,000 to 12,000, between 1980 and 1988, and the number of private motor cars, including those of the government, rose from 114,000 to 142,000 in the same period, an increase of some 30 percent. The number of telephones in use doubled between 1979 and 1988 from less than 90,000 to more than 180,000. Domestic mail traffic, as measured by the volume of letters handled, rose by 60 percent between 1980 and 1988, and so on. Other data point in the same direction, that internal movement and communication increased rapidly as a result of the improved infrastructure created by government programs (Kenya, 1991a,b).

Education

The achievements of the educational policy have been equally impressive and also highly visible. From 1976 to 1990, enrollment in primary schools in Kenya increased at an annual average rate of 4.4 percent. By 1990, primary school enrollment rates of the appropriate age cohorts were greater than 90 percent, with the enrollment rates for females only slightly lower than those for males. The number of primary schools roughly doubled during this same period, as did the number of teachers employed in the system (see Table 6-3). This expansion affected all parts of the country: The growth rates have been most rapid in the relatively remote districts of the northeast and west.

Expansion of the secondary school system has also been rapid but has not achieved the near-universality of the primary system. As might be expected, only a fraction of the primary school graduates go on to secondary school, but this fraction has been rising and as of 1990 stood at nearly half of the primary school graduates. Expansion of the secondary school system has been especially rapid in the last 10 years as the popularity of education has spread. Secondary school enrollments have been growing at about 5.0 percent per annum, more rapidly than primary school enrollments because of the lower base from which the former group started (Kenya, 1975, 1991a).

In both primary and secondary enrollments, the female proportion has tended to grow more rapidly than the male. In 1970, only about 40 percent of primary enrollees were females, but by 1991 this proportion had risen to 49 percent. There was substantial variations in this proportion by province, with the Coast and Western provinces in particular showing a much lower

TABLE 6-3 Growth of Social Programs in Kenya

	1970	1975	1980	1985	1990
Schools					
Primary			10,817	12,936	14,691
Secondary			1,904	2,413	2,654
Number of teachers			129,040	161,840	193,683
Doctors[a]	11.9	9.6	10.1	13.2	14.1
Registered and					
enrolled nurses[a]	63.7	72.8	97.2	102.7	107.5

[a]Per 100,000 population.

SOURCES: Kenya (1989b, 1991a).

female enrollment. Nationally, as of 1991 the proportion of females in the secondary school population was a lower 42 percent of the total.

Overall adult literacy has also grown steadily. Defined as the proportion of persons 15 years and older who are not students but who are literate, the proportion literate grew from 46 percent in 1976 to 54 percent in 1988. The rate of increase will climb sharply as the older age groups who passed through the school age years before the new policy was in effect die (Court and Ghai, 1974).

Health

Expansion of the health system has also been rapid (see Table 6-3). According to a recent World Bank (1991a) report, in 1960 Kenya had about 700 doctors, 2,000 registered nurses, and 11,000 hospital beds for a population of around 9 million. By 1969, the number of doctors and nurses had grown to more than 3,000 and 10,000, respectively, and the number of hospital beds had tripled. Since 1980, the number of all health facilities (hospitals, health centers, subcenters, and dispensaries) has increased by one-third with nearly all of this growth occurring among subcenters and dispensaries, particularly in rural areas. As of 1989, there was one health facility per 12,000 people in Kenya, and more than 75 percent of the population had a health facility within 8 kilometers of their residence. There are, of course, regional variations in these averages, and medical personnel do tend to concentrate in urban areas, but even the more remote areas are reasonably well served by the health system, particularly by African standards.

This system is public and private. About 70 percent of Kenya's hospital beds are provided in government facilities, and 70 percent of the rural health subcenters and dispensaries are operated by the Ministry of Health

(MOH) (Kenya, 1989c). Private institutions and practitioners, municipally sponsored facilities, and church-related or other nongovernmental organizations (NGOs) provide the rest. The emphasis of the system has been on curative medicine, but the MOH has also had considerable success with its child immunization program. By 1987, 75 percent of children aged 12 to 23 months had received the recommended three doses of oral polio and DPT (diphtheria-pertussis-tetanus) shots, and 60 percent had received the measles vaccine (Kenya, 1991c). Other preventive programs include child nutrition through growth monitoring and prenatal care. Health education and outreach programs have also been launched to deal with diarrheal diseases, stressing personal and household hygiene and safe water supply.

The system has clearly created a demand for its services. Underutilization of facilities, which is a common problem with new, rapidly expanding health systems in other developing countries, was never a problem in Kenya. Indeed, in 1989 the government initiated fees for nearly all of its health services, partly to force clients to become aware of the costs involved and not to overuse the services (and in the case of hospitals, to overstay).

Family Planning

Family planning services in Kenya have been delivered under the MOH, and this system has grown along with the health system. It is worthwhile to look at how family planning policy and program evolved in Kenya. In Kenya, as in many other developing countries, organized efforts to promote family planning began with privately sponsored associations in large cities, such as Nairobi and Mombasa, in the years just after World War II. A grant to the new Family Planning Association of Kenya (FPAK) from the Pathfinder Fund in 1959 allowed it to hire its first full-time organizer-secretary and to affiliate with the London-based International Planned Parenthood Federation (IPPF) in 1962, thus becoming the first sub-Saharan African affiliate of IPPF (Radel, 1973).

When Kenya became independent in 1963, the question of controlling population growth was, in a sense, already on the nation's agenda. As early as 1955, the East African Royal Commission on Land and Population had called attention to the rapid population growth and to the growing scarcity of new, arable land (Henin, 1985). The 1948 and 1962 population censuses documented the rapid growth in population and led to much discussion in the press. When, in 1965, the ruling government party issued its statement of national philosophy and purpose, the document expressed concern over the implications of unchecked population growth in Kenya. Shortly afterward, with technical and financial help from private foreign donor groups, most notably the Ford Foundation and the Population Council, the government invited a team of international experts to analyze the demographic situation in Kenya and make recommendations. This group's report, issued in August 1965, argued that rapid population growth was indeed a serious economic and social threat to Kenya's future, and urged a national policy and program to reduce fertility. The report was accepted by the cabinet after some spirited discussion and debate. It provided the basis for a similar analysis of population effects on development contained in the First Five-Year Development Plan adopted in 1966 and the announcement in 1967 of a National Family Planning Program. By 1968 the MOH had issued guidelines covering family planning to all its facilities and had opened the first explicitly family planning centers in the Central Province (Fendel and Gill, 1970; Radel, 1973; Henin, 1987).

Thus, only a few years after gaining independence, Kenya had adopted a national population program, making it the first country in sub-Saharan Africa to do so. This initiative inevitably raised hopes abroad that fertility reduction would follow quickly, but it did not. The Kenyan approach saw the family planning program effort as inescapably linked to the creation of a general rural health system; hence one could move only as fast as the other. Construction of facilities, training of staff, and procurement of equipment and supplies all had to precede effective delivery of services. A substantial amount of educational and public relations work was also required because in spite of the official policy there was great skepticism in and out of government about the need for the program. A data base and a capacity for program evaluation and research were built up slowly at the Central Bureau of Statistics and through the creation of the Population Studies and Research Institute at the University of Nairobi. This early, almost preliminary, period of building physical and human capital infrastructure consumed nearly the entire first decade of program activity.

Various organizational and administrative structures were proposed, employed, and then modified as program activity and experience grew. By 1982, program activity had become sufficiently multisectoral and complex to require a new overall coordinating body and the National Council on Population and Development (NCPD) was created (Henin, 1987; Oucho, 1987). The council's creation had strong support within the government of Kenya, including from President Moi himself, as well as from major foreign donor groups. The NCPD was not designed to replace the existing MOH service delivery network. It was created to coordinate the incorporation of other government agencies into the program, the expansion of private sector and NGO activities, and the development of a renewed public information and education emphasis (Saunders and Mbiti, 1979).

The 1980s, especially the last half, were the period during which the program began to take hold and show rapid growth. For example, between 1981-1982 and 1987-1988 the number of health workers trained in family planning grew from 1,027 to 2,170; the number of contraceptive service

delivery points (SDPs) increased from less than 100 to 465; and new accep-
tors increased from less than 100,000 annually to more than 300,000 (Henin,
1987). Two-thirds of this increase in trained health workers and four-fifths
of the openings of SDPs occurred during the latter half of the period. In the
last 2 years, the rate of training workers and creating SDPs accelerated
notably (Kelley and Nobbe, 1990). Private sector and NGO activity also
expanded rapidly. A private sector family planning project was launched in
1985, and a community-based contraceptive distribution scheme was initiated through FPAK in 1986. The privately sponsored Kenya Association
for Voluntary Sterilization began work in 1982 and grew rapidly (Bertrand
et al., 1989). All these agencies increased the outreach and also the popular
support for contraceptive usage (see Table 6-4) (Phillips and Kiragu, 1989).

Thus, it seems fair to say that in spite of early disappointments and a
series of premature and negative judgments from some observers, the Kenyan
family planning program had by the second half of the 1980s become an
effective mechanism for delivering services in Kenya. Its original strategy
of working through the growing health network appears to have been sound.
The program as it stands is by no means perfect, and its reach and influence
are uneven across the country. But one in three women in Kenya is now
contracepting, and some two-thirds of these women obtain their supplies
and other assistance from official service delivery points. The program is
an important part of why contraceptive prevalence is rising (Kelley and
Nobbe, 1990; Miller et al., 1991; World Bank, 1991b)

Land Policy

One other important facet of Kenyan government policy since independence remains to be discussed, namely, land policy. One of the first major
goals of the independent Kenyan government was to undo the longstanding
colonial government policy of reserving for white settlers some 3 million
acres of prize agricultural land in the rift valley and the highlands of north-
central Kenya. Between 1962 and 1972 a redistribution program, the "million acre scheme," was implemented and about 34,000 black Kenyans acquired land. These lands were purchased by the government and were
obtained either from white owners who were leaving the country or from
areas not being cultivated theretofore. Something less than a million acres
was actually transferred but the average new holding was still 20 acres, well
above the average of small subsistence farms in most regions of Kenya
(Okoth-Ogendo, 1981; Heyer et al., 1976; Bates, 1989).

The second stage of land redistribution was the creation of 12,000 Shiraka
plots, or farms, that gave the cultivator limited ownership and control subject to some traditional communal ownership rights. Many of the preexist-
ing white Kenyan farms took on black Kenyan coowners, and the white

TABLE 6-4   Kenya Family Planning Performance Data (thousands)

Year	First Visits	Revisits	Acceptors
1967	2	8	3
1968	12	18	9
1969	30	73	26
1970	35	114	31
1971	41	139	41
1972	45	172	43
1973	50	211	47
1974	51	233	49
1975	53	244	51
1976	61	272	53
1977	73	284	55
1978	62	303	67
1979	65	308	60
1980	65	350	61
1981	59	297	64
1982	65	344	63
1983	68	348	67
1984	83	370	82
1985	82	361	99
1986	93	366	92
1987	377	1,333	336
1988	257	682	251
1989	280	245	277

NOTE: The coverage of the data collection system varies from year to year, thus, year-to-year changes should not be interpreted too literally. However, we believe the trends indicated are broadly reliable.

SOURCES: Krystall et al. (1978); Kenya (1989d).

monopoly on the most fertile land effectively ended. However, a dualistic pattern of land holdings has persisted in Kenyan agriculture, with one-quarter of the high- and medium-potential arable land being farmed in large units that produce more than half of all agricultural output (Bates, 1989). The remaining one-half of total output is produced by small-scale farms on three-quarters of the high- and medium-potential land plus the low-potential land, which is four times as large as the richer-grade land. Thus, 20 percent of the farms, occupying 5 percent of the total arable land, produce half of the total agricultural output. This half is the major exportable surplus that flows to the urban areas and abroad.

Along with the land redistribution policies the government attempted to rationalize the pattern of land tenure through the "registration, adjudication, and consolidation program." The program was an effort to provide legally correct, secure, freehold tenure for individual owners so that they would be encouraged to invest in the land and, hence, increase productivity and output. The old communal holding system and growing land squatting were thought to militate against increases in agricultural productivity. To this end, land surveys were undertaken, and a legal procedure for obtaining clear titles, as well as procedures for settling disputes, was established. These processes continue into the early 1990s but have not by all means eliminated disputes or led to a clear understanding regarding ownership of all land (Okoth-Ogendo, 1981).

On balance, the World Bank and other observers believe that land has been more widely distributed in Kenya in the last several decades (World Bank, 1980, 1983). The nationalization scheme has, however, been a mixed blessing for smallholders because frequently the procedures for obtaining title favor the wealthy and the better educated at the expense of the real cultivators. Land prices have risen, leading some smallholders to sell unwisely simply to support current consumption. All in all, landlessness has probably increased (Harbeson, 1971; Collier and Lal, 1980; World Bank, 1983).

Overall, these land policies have had the effect of increasing output and broadening the base of ownership, but have done little to aid the smallholder or the landless. The sheer weight of population increase alone would cause rising land prices and pressure on all existing holdings. Kenya's population has roughly doubled since independence, whereas cultivable land has increased little if at all. Limited evidence suggests that Kenyans are aware of these changing circumstances. Scarcity of land was cited as one of the primary motives for voluntary surgical contraception in four districts in Kenya (Bertrand et al., 1989). Focus group studies by Hammerslough (1991a) indicate that lack of arable land was a key factor in the decision to use contraception.

EFFECTS OF GOVERNMENT INITIATIVES ON FERTILITY

Let us now return to the decision process by which fertility has been led to decline in Kenya. We have suggested that once controlled fertility becomes the norm and replaces natural fertility, couples attempt a purposeful balancing of the expected gains and losses (or benefits and costs) from various family sizes and then act accordingly, using whatever controlling technology is available to them. Coale has interpreted the essence of what goes on in a fertility transition as three interrelated steps (Coale, 1973). First, couples must come to understand and fully accept that fertility can be controlled (without physical or moral harm to anyone); second, couples must then desire control over their own fertility, plan, and act accordingly; third, couples must have access to some means of effecting control and implementing their plans, which promises a reasonable probability of success. Coale has called this the "ready, willing, and able" rule, and we can view the economic model as becoming applicable when people come to understand that control is possible, desirable, and feasible. The economic model centers on the desirability aspect and articulates the various factors that affect the benefits and costs of children and hence the "demand" for them. What most family planning programs are all about is making it easier for couples to plan and implement their fertility goals effectively (Berelson, 1977).

Thus, the thrust of a great deal of Kenya's development effort has been toward the creation of better social infrastructure and improving the quality of the human capital stock. In a single generation, Kenyans have become literate, geographically mobile, consumer goods-oriented, health-seeking economic beings. In short, they have experienced a profound change in basic orientation, attitudes, and aspirations. Government policy has contributed to this transformation in the following specific ways:

1. Achieving near-universal primary school enrollment has resulted in mass literacy for the below-40 age groups being achieved and a strong desire for still-higher education being implanted in nearly all households. Literacy affects fertility in a variety of ways including opening couples to new ideas and new information, increasing modern sector labor force participation of both men and women, and leading to an aspiration for fewer, but higher-quality (better-educated) children. The actual approach to education pursued by the government has been a cost-sharing one. That is, although no fees are charged for primary school enrollment, the villagers are responsible typically for building and maintaining the schools, and must also bear the cost of textbooks, supplies, and uniforms, which can be substantial, particularly for a large family. This cost sharing has served as a constant reminder that there is an out-of-pocket cost connected with children for the parents. In addition, primary schooling has been mandatory since 1978.

2. The large government investment in the health system has helped reduce the level of mortality and morbidity, particularly among infants and young children. Couples in Kenya are now aware that most children born will survive to adulthood and hence there is less need for "excess" births to achieve any given target of family size. The growth of the government health system, with the parallel NGO network, has also had the effect of building confidence in the usefulness of such services. When the clinics and personnel are there and are helpful, people tend to return and to become "health seekers." Because of the close link between the family planning program and the general health system, the growth of public confidence in the health system has paid substantial dividends for the family planning effort as well.

new ideas, increased employment in the modern sector, and contributed to smaller desired family sizes as parents invest in the education of fewer children.   Expansion of the health care system has undoubtedly reduced infant and child mortality rates and inspired public acceptance of the usefulness of health, as well as family planning, services.   Improvements in physical infrastructure have connected most communities with the modern sector and increased the flows of people and ideas.   Finally, these programs have not neglected women and have probably contributed to their improved status.

7

Linkages Between Socioeconomic Factors and Demographic Change

In this chapter, we attempt to link socioeconomic factors to changes in child mortality and fertility. In the first two sections, we investigate these links at the district level. We also discuss the relation of child mortality to adult mortality and to fertility. Finally, we analyze contraceptive use at the individual level using a multivariate model.

CHILD MORTALITY AND SOCIOECONOMIC FACTORS

The most notable finding from the analysis of child mortality trends in Chapter 3 is the consistency of the changes over time for subregions (provinces and districts) from the 1950s onward. Despite the difficulties of determining precisely the level of child mortality in the later 1980s, it can be deduced with confidence that the rates continued to fall at a pace similar to the previous decade. This continuation was established for the country and the provinces (excluding the thinly populated Northeastern Province). The changes by districts in the most recent period cannot yet be estimated, but the regularity of the district child mortality declines prior to the 1970s, and the continuance of the province trends into the 1980s, make it certain that similar conclusions can be drawn about all, or almost all, of the smaller aggregates. The child mortality reductions of 1954 to 1974, given in Chapter 3, are then satisfactory indices of the subregional improvements. The estimation methods, which use the proportion of children dead by age groups of mothers from census reports, are capable of producing sufficiently accurate values for the broad levels of child mortality in given periods but not precise measures by stages of childhood or calendar years. This conclusion follows because the dead children of women in any age group are spread over a range of dates of births and deaths.

Cross-Sectional Relationships

The information for the calculation of child mortality up to the 1970s has been available for some years. There are several examinations of the relations between the mortality estimates and the socioeconomic indices for provinces and districts. The most relevant for the present study are by Ewbank et al. (1986) and Blacker et al. (1987). In both of these, the child mortality estimates were derived by essentially the same techniques used in the present report. There are slight differences in detail, according to the measures employed (e.g., infant mortality in Ewbank et al.) and the location in time. There are also variations in the methods of adjusting the estimates in the small number of cases where the data are suspect. These divergences have a negligible impact on the investigation of socioeconomic linkages at the attainable level of precision. The main concern of these two papers was with the cross-sectional district variations at points of time, although there is some attempt to look at changes. The emphasis here is on determinants of trends. The two issues are, of course, closely linked but far from identical. For example, the basic environmental factors associated with particular causes of death, such as malaria, are likely to appear more prominently in cross-sectional investigations.

Ewbank et al. (1986) reported the results of a regression analysis of district infant mortality rates from the 1969 and 1979 censuses and the intercensal changes. The explanatory variables included for the 1979 exercise were female literacy, the prevalence of malaria, the percentage urban, the number of kilometers of road, the population density, and the potential agricultural land per capita. A measure of availability of health services was constructed from the per capita availability of beds in hospitals and dispensaries, divided by the square root of the land area of the district. There were also a series of variables that assigned each district to one of five ecological zones. A similar analysis was applied to the infant mortality estimates from the 1969 census, but two variables—number of kilometers of road and prevalence of malaria—were omitted because of lack of data. In the regression analysis of change, the ecological zones were included along with the 1969 to 1979 differences for the other available variables.

Several relations significant at the 10 percent level of probability were determined. In both 1969 and 1979, infant mortality was lower in districts with higher proportions of educated females age 25-29, with greater population densities, and with more high-potential agricultural land. Nyanza and Western provinces in the ecological zone defined by the Lake Victoria basin experienced significantly high infant mortality rates as did, to a lesser extent, the dry eastern and coastal areas (Coast Province plus Kitui and Machakos districts). A substantial part of the district infant mortality variation was accounted for by the socioeconomic and environmental variables (the R^2 coefficients were .70 and .80 for the 1969 and 1979 analyses, respectively). However, the analysis of changes in infant mortality between 1969 and 1979 revealed only a weak relation with the independent variables (R^2 equaled .26), the only significant factors being the percentage of educated females among those aged 25-29 years and a slightly better performance in the Nyanza and Western provinces ecological zone.

Ewbank and colleagues also utilized the reports on malnutrition in the third Kenya nutrition survey in 1982. The prevalence of stunting (short heights at given ages of children) is an indicator of chronic malnutrition. Children were classed as stunted if their heights were less than 90 percent of the World Health Organization (WHO) standard. The proportions stunted in each district were added as a variable in the regression analysis for 1979 already described. The extra contribution to the explanation of the mortality variation was negligible. A reduced multiple regression retaining only the female education and stunting variables resulted in both having significant effects at the 5 percent level, with 50 percent of the variation in infant mortality accounted for. However, when the proportion of outpatient cases due to malaria was included in the regression, the stunting association became nonsignificant. It appears that a complex of socioeconomic and environmental factors contributed to the district variations in child mortality, but the parts played by each cannot be disentangled.

National-level differentials in child mortality figures and trends by education of the mother are presented and discussed in Chapter 3. The 1979 census provided data on proportions of children dead by age group of mothers, subdivided by both district and education. Measures of child mortality can be derived from these proportions by the same methods applied previously for the district totals. Kibet (1981) provided such measures using the index $_2q_0$ (the probability of death in the first 2 years of life), which is obtained by a slight modification of the proportions of children dead for mothers aged 20-24 years. For Kenya as a whole, the $_2q_0$ for women with a secondary education was only 37 percent of the corresponding value for women with no education. In the great majority of districts the ratio did not vary much from the national average. In some of the more remote areas where it did, the numbers of women with a secondary education were low and the sample errors large. The broad regularity of the relation can be illustrated from the districts with the lowest overall $_2q_0$, Nyeri, and the highest, South Nyanza. In the former, the secondary education mortality index is 39 percent of the no-schooling value; in the latter, the proportion is 43 percent. As pointed out by Ewbank et al., this result suggests that the relation between maternal education and child mortality is not an artifact of environmental factors or cultural characteristics. As they noted, however, education is not the only important determinant because women with secondary education in South Nyanza had a higher $_2q_0$ (.104) than the uneducated in Nyeri (.079). Similar reversals apply in many comparisons between pairs of districts from the upper and lower ranges of child mortality.

Although Blacker et al. (1987) used much the same measures as Ewbank and colleagues, their approach was different. They examined, using scatter diagrams, how district variations in child mortality (as described by $_5q_0$) related to single socioeconomic and environmental measures. Their aim was to illuminate the nature of the associations by highlighting deviant districts. The causes of the deviation could have been biases in the measures due to data errors or real differences in the patterns among subregions of the country. Blacker and colleagues found that many of the relations explored produced no signs of significant interactions. The only variables to which child mortality was related were female education, percentage of outpatients with malaria, stunting (less than 90 percent of the WHO height-age standard), wasting (less than 80 percent of the WHO weight-age standard), percentage of households with no piped water, persons per health facility, and population density.

Although there were suggestions of correlations between child mortality shortly before the 1979 census and health indicators, none is very impressive except that with the prevalence of malaria. The stunting and wasting indices derived from the Third Rural Nutrition Survey of 1982 tended to be large in the high-mortality districts of the Coast Province and small for the low-mortality Central Province. But over the bulk of the districts there was little association, and the diagrams showed a wide scatter with only a slight tendency for the $_5q_0$ values to increase with the stunting and wasting proportions. The configuration of the plot for $_5q_0$ and the percentage of households without piped water (also derived from the 1982 Nutrition Survey) were very similar to the stunting and wasting results, although with notable deviations in some districts. Thus, some of the highest child mortality areas of the Coast were classified as good in terms of water supply. Because only a small proportion of households had piped water, however, the analysis was not a powerful one. The persons per health facility (hospitals, health centers, clinics, and dispensaries) in each district were weighted by the square root of the land area to obtain an "access" variable for 1979. The overall plot of child mortality against the health facility access variable indicated no association but if the small number of outliers (five) with extremely high (i.e., poor) access measures but average mortality were ignored, some tendency for improvement with better access emerged. Again the relation came largely from the favorable position of the Central Province districts and the unfavorable placing of some coastal regions.

The examination of how child mortality varied with population density did not reveal very much. The $_5q_0$ values were high in the densely populated districts bordering Lake Victoria but low in the equally congested areas of Central Province. In some of the districts of low density, for example, on the coast, a large proportion of the population was settled in subregions that, if the data could be disaggregated, would show much increased measures of persons per unit area.

The increase in $_5q_0$ with the percentage of new outpatients with malaria was consistent and convincing. The scatter diagram is reproduced in Figure 7-1. Although the index of malaria prevalence was less than ideal, Blacker et al. note that it agreed well with spleen enlargement rates where these were available. Only three districts seem to fit distinctly poorly with the apparent relation of $_5q_0$ to the malaria prevalence index. In two of these, Baringo and Kisii, there was reason to doubt the validity of the malaria measures because they were not consistent with spleen rates. The latter implied levels that would improve agreement with the regression line. The largest proportion of new outpatients with malaria was recorded for Bungoma where child mortality was high but rather lower than expected on the basis of the correlation.

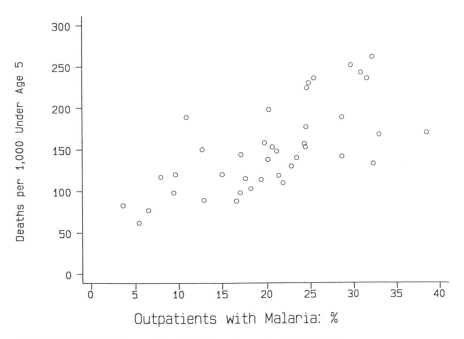

FIGURE 7-1   Child mortality (1974) and malaria (1975-1984).

The large differentials in childhood mortality by education of the mother are noted in Chapter 3 of this report and are documented in many studies of Kenya. The analogous relation for district aggregates appeared in the Ewbank et al. (1986) multivariate analyses of the 1969 and 1979 census estimates. The Blacker et al. (1987) scatter diagram by districts for 1979 of $_5q_0$ plotted against the percentage of women aged 15 years or more with no schooling was consistent with the other findings. However, in districts with lower levels of female educational attainment, the association was far from regular. There were two clusters that were inconsistent with the relationship shown by the other units. In four districts of the Lake Victoria basin (Kisumu, Siaya, South Nyanza, and Busia), child mortality was exceptionally high but education levels were near average. In a group of districts in the thinly populated areas of northern Kenya plus Narok and Kajiado on the border with Tanzania, educational levels were low but mortality was estimated to be moderate. The latter cluster included several of the districts where there was most doubt about the accuracy of child mortality estimates, but the view that there may be favorable environmental factors to offset the adverse effects of poorly educated mothers in these districts is not implausible. Blacker et al. also calculated the ratio of $_5q_0$ from the 1979 census to the corresponding value from the 1969 census and plotted results by district against the improvements in female education (measured as the proportion of women over 15 years with no education in 1979, divided by the corresponding proportion in 1969). Although the points were widely scattered, particularly where the improvements in education were small or even retrograde, there was a distinct relationship. Again, it tended to be dominated by the districts of Central Province, where there were substantial gains in female education and child mortality, and the coast plus the more remote northern areas where changes in both were small.

Relationships with Trends

Most of the association of child mortality with socioeconomic indicators investigated by Ewbank et al. and by Blacker et al. were at certain points in time (mainly around 1979). But the emphasis in the present study is on trends. Therefore, we have focused on comparing the mortality declines and socioeconomic measures by district. The data utilized are essentially the same as in the other analyses, although there are some differences in specification. The conceptual framework is, however, a little different. The mortality trends are taken to represent a process of change that operated consistently from the 1950s to the present. The socioeconomic indicators measured late in that period are assumed to reflect the development over the range of time in the relevant sectors: education of women, provision of health services, etc. In Figure 7-2, the district child mortality de-

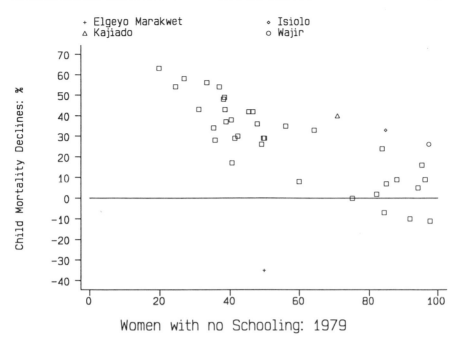

FIGURE 7-2   Child mortality declines (1954-1974) and female education (1979).

clines from the mid-1950s to the mid-1970s are plotted against the percentages of women aged 15-44 years with no schooling as reported in the 1979 census. Nairobi and Mombasa were excluded because of obvious selection problems due to their large movements in population. The association between the two variables is apparent. The districts that deviate from the general regression (Kajiado, Isiolo, Wajir, and Elgeyo-Marakwet) are remoter areas for which there is some doubt about the reliability of the mortality estimates. However, it is also possible that environmental factors are affecting the death rates differently there than in the rest of the country. The group of districts in the lake basin that were outliers in the relation between child mortality level in 1979 and female education (Kisumu, Siaya, South Nyanza, and Busia) now fit in well, because the mortality decreases are moderate as is educational attainment, although the death rates were high at all points of time. Several of the more remote areas with a small proportion of educated women, but moderate child mortality, recorded only a slight fall in the latter or even a rise (Garissa, Turkana, Marsabit, Samburu, and Mandera). Thus, the association of the trends in child mortality with the level of female education reached in 1979 is clearer and tidier than the cross-sectional relations found in the earlier studies. A similar exercise,

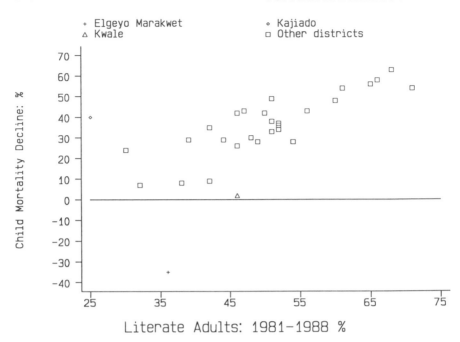

FIGURE 7-3   Child mortality declines (1954-1974) and adult literacy (1981-1988).

with the percentage of females among pupils at secondary schools as the education variable, also indicates a fair correlation—but less impressive than demonstrated by Figure 7-2.

It seems likely that the mortality declines by district would also be associated with adult literacy, and this relation is confirmed by Figure 7-3. The literacy data are taken from the Rural Literacy Surveys of 1981 and 1988. The indicator used is an average of the proportions of adults classed as literate (both sexes) in 1981 and 1988. Literacy was defined in the surveys as the ability to read and write in any language. The average was taken to reduce sample errors and individuals biases. Although in most districts the change from 1981 to 1988 was small or plausible, there were notable exceptions, for example, Narok (20 percent in 1981, 39 percent in 1988) and Kwale (57 percent in 1981, 35 percent in 1988). Only 30 districts were available for the plotting of points because of the exclusion of urban areas such as Nairobi and Mombasa and some amalgamation of remote districts. The regularity of the association between mortality improvement and higher adult literacy is impressive. The outlying points are for Elgeyo-Marakwet, where the estimated trend in child mortality is hard to believe, Kwale, and Kajiado. If the more plausible 1988 measure of adult literacy is taken for Kwale, it is no longer an outlier. The fact that adult literacy (covering both sexes) is as closely related to the child mortality trend as female education is, suggests that the associations are the product of general rather than specific influences.

Exploration of the links of socioeconomic variables with fertility decreases, presented later in this chapter, suggests that female employment might be related to child mortality as well. The numbers of women employed in the modern sector in each district were taken from the employment survey and divided by the corresponding total women aged 15-44 years in the district at the 1979 census. The coverage of the employment survey is by no means complete, and the age range of women workers is not restricted to 15-44 years. Nor will employment always be in the district of residence, particularly near urban areas such as Nairobi and Mombasa. Nevertheless, the indices give a rough guide to the intensity of female employment in the modern sector. The declines in child mortality by district are plotted against the female employment measures in Figure 7-4. Our hypothesis is that the greater exposure to external ideas through employment in the modern sector is favorable to the spread of healthier child care practices. The scatter diagram indicates an association, but it is far from linear

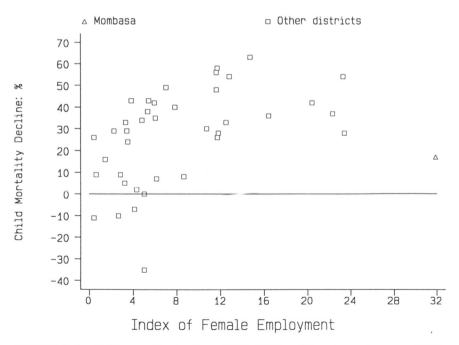

FIGURE 7-4   Child mortality declines (1954-1974) and female employment (1980).

and is determined mainly by the Central Province districts with large child mortality improvements and fairly high employment indices, as well as those districts with poor mortality declines and low female employment. The latter are geographically spread in Coast, Rift Valley, Northeastern, and Eastern provinces. When the female employment index exceeds 5 percent (27 of the 40 points, excluding Nairobi), there is little, if any, rise in the improvement of child mortality with the employment measure.

The lack of much relation between child mortality in the late 1970s and the availability of health facilities was noted by Blacker et al. In Figure 7-5, the same health facility indicator is plotted against child mortality trends. Again, there is little relation between the variables, except that provided by the Central Province districts with the five largest mortality declines and good provision of health services. If these are omitted, the correlation becomes negligible. Whatever association exists is due to a coincidence of developments in a limited region of the country. Much the same conclusions apply to the relations between child mortality trends and other health indicators, namely, the prevalence of malaria and of wasting and stunting, as well as the availability of piped water. For all of these indicators, the Central districts have favorable measures. The nutritional indicators are

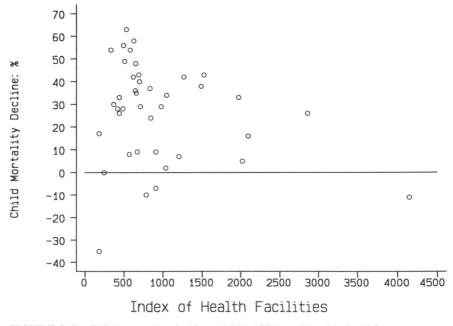

FIGURE 7-5   Child mortality declines (1954-1974) and health facilities.

poor for the Coast districts, which also show little fall in child mortality. For the other districts, the plots show a wide scatter of points with little correlation. The configuration of the graphs provides no support for the claim that these socioeconomic factors are significantly related to falls in child mortality.

Relationship with Adult Mortality

In Chapter 3 the relation between adult and childhood mortality levels is examined briefly, following Blacker et al. (1987). As pointed out, the only usable data are for the 1969 to 1979 census interval, and therefore the emphasis on longer-term trends in childhood mortality cannot be pursued for adults. Blacker et al. also examined relations of adult mortality levels estimated for 1969-1979 to population density and to female education by district. The former exercise revealed little. As would be expected from the association between child mortality and female education as demonstrated by Ewbank et al. (1986) and Blacker et al. (1987), and the association between child and adult mortality, higher levels of life expectancy at age 15, $e(15)$, tended to be associated with more schooling. The correlation was modest, however, and somewhat weaker than the link between child mortality trends and female education. It is true that the northern districts with their low adult life expectancies and poor schooling fit in well with the regression, but there were outliers scattered over the provinces (e.g., Kisumu, Taita-Taveta, Narok, and Kilifi). A plot of the $e(15)$ measures against the percentage of women with no schooling is shown in Figure 7-6. In view of the measurement uncertainties, it would be unjustified to conclude that female education was more closely related to child than to adult mortality. Rather, the education index reflects factors that are significant for both.

FERTILITY AND SOCIOECONOMIC FACTORS

The extensive previous analyses of fertility in Kenya have focused on cross-sectional variations in levels and patterns of fertility in relation to socioeconomic and environmental influences. There have also been some attempts to examine the causes of the increases in fertility in the 1950s and 1960s. But evidence of declining fertility in the 1980s became available only with the dissemination of the data from the 1988-1989 Kenya Demographic and Health Survey (KDHS). Thus, there has been no analysis of the relation of the declines to socioeconomic factors. The extraction of reliable measures of the fertility decreases for aggregates smaller than provinces is not straightforward. The estimates made in Chapter 4 for 17 districts out of the 41 total (comprising about two-thirds of the population) are clearly not precise but can be used with caution to explore relations to socioeconomic

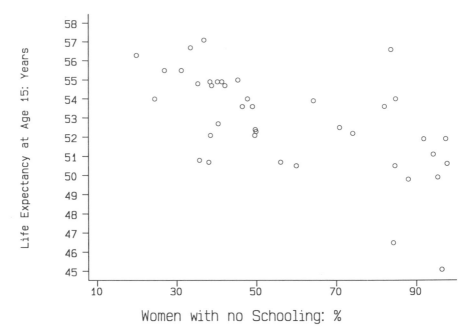

FIGURE 7-6 Adult mortality (life expectancy at age 15, 1969-1979) and female education (1979).

indicators. Some estimates have been marked as particularly doubtful on the basis of supplementary evidence, and these concerns should be remembered in assessment of the associations.

The measures of fertility declines at the district level are taken from the comparison of birth rates by age of woman in the 5 years preceding the KDHS and for the period 5 to 10 years before the survey. These rates were calculated from the birth histories. The rates by age were cumulated up to age 40 years, the highest possible for the earlier period because of the truncation as the time location receded into the past. The measures compared are thus not complete total fertility rates, but the distinction is trivial at the level of precision practicable. The relations between these measures of fertility decline and the socioeconomic and health indicators utilized in the examination of child mortality trends are explored below. Few associations of any note are found. It is true that the number of units is small (16 when Nairobi is excluded, which is normally the case because of the mobility of the population). The measures have substantial uncertainty and possibly systematic errors. Nevertheless, the range of variation is considerable, and strong associations should be detectable. Measures of fertility change are not available for the remote districts with small populations, but it may be speculated that any reductions would be small because in general, these are also the areas with poor social development. Their omission from the assessment of association, therefore, probably removes from the graphs sets of points that would tend to increase correlations. It seems unlikely, however, that this omission is of much specific significance, and there is a case for treating the more remote areas as being in a separate conceptual universe for the interpretation of relationships.

The relation of educational indices to decreases in child mortality, as well as the fertility differentials by length of schooling, make further investigation of the interactions of education with fertility declines an obvious place to start. Figure 7-7 plots these declines by district from the mid-1970s to the mid-1980s against the percentage of women aged 15-44 years with no schooling as recorded at the 1979 census. It is evident that there is no indication of a relation between the two variables. Only one district with a low level of schooling (Kilifi) appears on the graph, where it is very much an outlier in educational level but its fertility decline is near average. It is worth noting that a plot of child mortality declines against the percentage of women with no schooling, confined to the 16 districts of Figure 7-7,

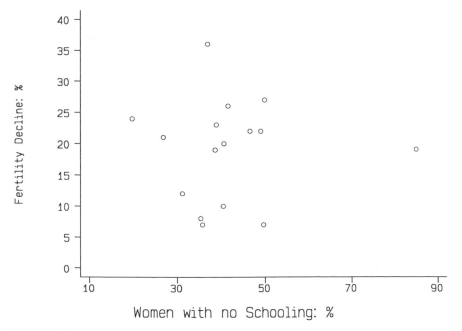

FIGURE 7-7 Fertility declines (1974-1978 to 1984-1988) and female education (1979).

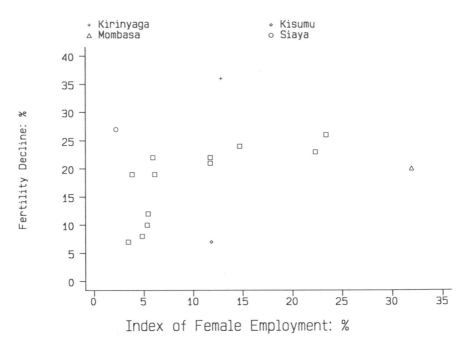

FIGURE 7-8   Fertility declines (1974-1978 to 1984-1988) and female employment in the modern sector (1980), selected districts and rest of Kenya.

preserves the strong relation of the former variable to the latter, as in the larger array of districts in Figure 7-2.

Figure 7-8 shows the plot of fertility declines against the index constructed for female employment in the modern sector, and Figure 7-9 shows the corresponding graph for male employment in the modern sector. The employment indices for Mombasa and Kisumu (Nairobi is omitted) are probably too high because of the problem of employees from outside the district working in these urban areas. Siaya is an anomaly, but the strong doubts about the estimated fertility decline for this district have already been emphasized. When these reservations are allowed, there appears to be a consistent and fairly regular increase in the fertility decrease as the index of female employment increases.[1] Not surprisingly, the correlation between the female and male indices of employment is high, and Figure 7-9 has much the same configuration as Figure 7-8. It seems odd that the fertility declines are correlated with the level of female employment in the modern

---

[1]We have no evidence of the direction of causation in the relationship between female employment and fertility change. Employment in the modern sector may be affected by fertility and vice versa.

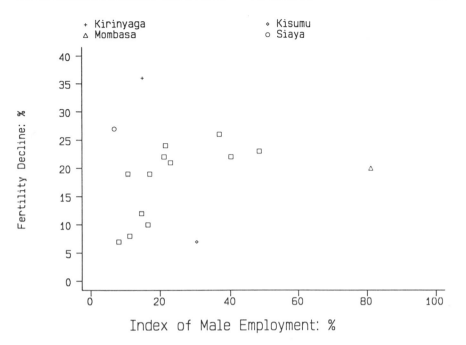

FIGURE 7-9 Fertility declines (1974-1978 to 1984-1988) and male employment in the modern sector (1980), selected districts and rest of Kenya.

sector but so little associated with the schooling of women. An inspection of the corresponding indices of female employment and schooling reveals that in the "remote" districts, the measures are both quite low. However, there is little correlation elsewhere, and the estimated fertility declines largely exclude the remote category. In the coastal districts where the education level is very low but fertility falls are moderate, female employment is on the low side but not extremely so.

CHILD MORTALITY LINKAGES WITH FERTILITY DECLINES

The demographic changes in Kenya provide particular opportunities for an exploration of the contribution made by the child mortality reductions to the declines in fertility. It has long been widely assumed that the former is a major stimulus or prerequisite of the latter, in conformity with classic transition theory, although firm quantitative support has been limited (Preston, 1977). In Kenya, the fertility decline occurred abruptly and was expected by few observers; it was proximately determined by the adoption of family planning, rather than by alterations in the size and composition of the population at risk for childbearing. The novelty and sharpness of the effect in a country where previously there had been much concern about rising fertility define the phenomenon to be explained with unusual clarity. There are equally favorable characteristics of the changes in child mortality. The trends were remarkably regular within provinces and districts from the 1950s to the 1970s, and there is convincing evidence that they continued similarly into the 1980s. The information on improvements in child mortality, up to and including the period of the fertility decline, can therefore be captured by one measure for each district.

Table 7-1 brings together the estimates of child mortality trends by provinces and districts (the decrease in $_5q_0$ from 1954 to 1974) and the fertility declines between 1974-1978 and 1984-1988 derived from the KDHS birth histories. The estimated $_5q_0$ values around 1974 are also shown, as are the direct measures for provinces of the declines between the total fertilities in the preceding 5 years, which are based on data from KFS and KDHS.

TABLE 7-1   Child Mortality and Fertility Trends by Province and District

	$_5q_0$		Fertility Decline (%)	
Province/District	1974	1954-1974 Decline (%)	1974-1978 to 1984-1988	1973-1977 to 1984-1988
Central	.085	56	27	31
Kirinyaga	.117	54	36	
Muranga	.089	58	21	
Nyeri	.062	63	24	
Coast	.199	11	21	27
Kilifi	.236	7	19	
Mombasa	.140	17	20	
Eastern	.125	40	13	16
Machakos	.119	43	12	
Meru	.103	42	22	
Nyanza	.217	34	13	13
Kisii	.133	43	19	
Kisumu	.243	28	7	
Siaya	.252	29	27	
South Nyanza	.262	29	7	
Rift Valley	.132	21	23	20
Kericho	.115	26	22	
Nakuru	.120	37	23	
Uasin Gishu	.114	28	26	
Western	.186	34	1	4
Bungoma	.170	34	8	
Kakamega	.168	38	10	
Nairobi	.102	16	14	26

At the province level the association between child mortality and fertility declines is far from impressive. Although Central Province ranks first in the size of both reductions, the poor mortality improvements for the Rift Valley and especially the Coast Province are set against substantial declines in fertility. Indeed the Coast Province recorded the second highest fertility decline in the comparison of the directly calculated KDHS and KFS measures.

If the districts are arranged by the size of the mortality declines, the ordering of the corresponding fertility declines is far from being in close accordance. It is true that the Central Province districts with the largest mortality decreases (Nyeri, Muranga, and Kirinyaga) all have substantial fertility reductions, but other areas with modest mortality improvements have fertility declines of the same order (Nakuru and Uasin Gishu). Machakos and Kakamega, which do quite well in lowered mortality, have very modest declines in fertility. The most striking discrepancies, however, are for the Coast Province. Kilifi and Mombasa, with substantial fertility reductions of around 20 percent, had the two smallest mortality declines in the sample of districts. The residual fertility decreases for the Coast Province districts not shown separately is estimated at around 20 percent. One of these, Taita-Taveta, had a large child mortality decrease of 48 percent, but it contained only one-quarter of the combined population (aggregated with Kwale, Lamu, and Tana River). For these, the mortality declines were all less than 2 percent. It seems clear that strong fertility decreases were associated with close to zero mortality reductions in most of the coastal districts.

Remarks of a similar nature, although varying in detail, can be made if the mortality level around 1974 rather than the trend in mortality is considered. Thus, the districts of Kilifi, Kwale, Lamu, and Tana River in Coast Province had $_5q_0$ measures of 189 to 236 per 1,000, but apparently substantial fertility declines. Machakos combined low mortality with a modest fertility decline. It may be noted that child mortality up to age 5 years in Central Province in 1954 was lower than that of Coast in 1974, with the mid-1980s level of the latter probably little different. Nevertheless, the fertility decline did not occur significantly earlier in the former province.

In Figure 7-10, the percentage fertility declines are plotted against the child mortality trends for districts. The lack of consistent relation is clearly illustrated. It is possible, and indeed likely, that the steady decline in childhood mortality from the 1950s and earlier contributed to the awareness of changing social conditions and, hence, to fertility declines. But there is no support for the view that they were an important immediate, direct, and specific influence, at least as measured at the district level. The timing and geographical correlations are quite inconsistent with such an interpretation.

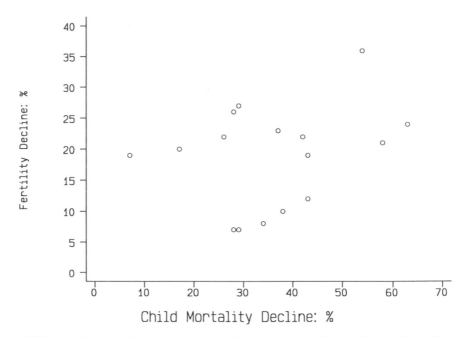

FIGURE 7-10   Fertility and child mortality declines (fertility: 1974-1977 to 1984-1988; mortality: 1954-1974).

MULTIVARIATE ANALYSIS OF CONTRACEPTIVE USE

The analysis of the proximate determinants of fertility in Chapter 5 demonstrates that the decline in fertility between the 1977-1978 KFS and 1988-1989 KDHS was due primarily to an increase in contraceptive use. Therefore, in order to understand the factors underlying the change in fertility, it is essential to understand the factors associated with increased contraceptive use. This section seeks to highlight the individual- and community-level characteristics associated with contraceptive use in Kenya.

Methodology

Ideally, one would want to analyze the trends in contraceptive use between the two surveys. Unfortunately, the data from the KFS are not disaggregated at the district level, which makes it impossible to link district-level characteristics to individual-level data. However, because contraceptive use was so low at the time of the KFS, levels of use at the time of the KDHS are fairly representative of trends and serve as an adequate proxy for changes that occurred between the two surveys.

A logistic regression is used to analyze the factors associated with contraceptive use. The dependent variable indicates whether or not a woman is currently using contraception. The sample includes nonpregnant women currently in a union. Individual-level characteristics from the KDHS and district-level characteristics taken from various government surveys and documents are used as explanatory variables.[2]

Results

The results of the analysis are presented in Table 7-2. Most of the factors operate on contraceptive use as expected. Availability of family planning demonstrates the strongest positive association with contraceptive use. A woman living in a district with at least 11 service delivery points (SDPs) per 100,000 people is 2.75 times as likely to use contraception as a woman living in a district with fewer than 11 SDPs per 100,000 people, net of other individual- and district-level effects. Density of family planning services clearly has a positive effect on increased contraceptive use, either by providing the means to attain limited family size or by introducing the concept of fertility control not previously considered by the woman.

Hammerslough (1991a) gave evidence for the former explanation in an analysis of survey data from the Kenya Community Survey, which was conducted in 1989 in 260 of the rural sample clusters used in the KDHS. This survey gathered community information from adult residents, including information on family planning service availability. Using a multivariate framework, he concluded that although accessibility to services increased at the same time as demand for contraception rose, it did not initiate the increase in contraception. However, the increased availability of services probably did induce more women to use efficient methods instead of traditional ones.

Interestingly, at the individual level, family planning accessibility, as measured by a woman's travel time to a family planning source, is not significantly associated with contraceptive use. This result is not totally

---

[2]The sources of community-level data for the multivariate analysis are as follows:

• number of service delivery points by district, 1991: Health Information System Unit, Ministry of Health computer file, November, 1991;
• kilometers of paved road per 10,000 people, 1991: provided by the Roads Department in the Ministry of Transportation and Communication;
• percentage of the rural population literate, 1988: Kenya (1990);
• percentage of the female population employed in the modern sector, 1980: employment data from 1980 Kenya employment survey divided by women aged 15-44 years at the 1979 census; and
• percentage of the district that is urban, 1989: Kenya (1991b).

TABLE 7-2   Logit Estimates of Probability of Contraceptive Use Among Nonpregnant Women Currently in Union, Kenya, 1989

Explanatory Variables	β	SE(β)	Odds Ratio
Individual Level			
Travel time to family planning source			
(More than one hour)			
Less than one hour	.001	.094	1.00
Household electricity			
(No electricity)			
Electricity	.972[a]	.184	2.64
Education			
(None)			
1-6 years	.317[a]	.114	1.37
7+ years	.658[a]	.117	1.93
Type of household flooring			
(Mud floor)			
Other than mud floor	.497[a]	.103	1.64
Woman's group			
(Does not belong)			
Belongs	.365[a]	.087	1.44
Listens to radio			
(Less than once a week)			
At least once a week	.306[a]	.099	1.36
Type of residence			
(Rural)			
Urban	−.477[a]	.155	0.62
Age			
(15-24)			
25-39	.621[a]	.116	1.86
40+	.567[a]	.147	1.76
Religion			
(Muslim or other)			
Christian	.290	.195	1.34
District Level			
Availability of family planning			
(Fewer than 11 service			
delivery points per 100,000 people)			
At least 11 service delivery			
points per 100,000 people	1.012[a]	.145	2.75
Rural literacy			
(Less than 50% of the rural			
population literate)			
At least 50% of the rural			
population literate	.973[a]	.124	2.65

continued

TABLE 7-2 *Continued*

Explanatory Variables	β	SE(β)	Odds Ratio
Paved roads			
(Fewer than 25 kilometers			
of paved road per 10,000 people)			
At least 25 kilometers of			
paved road per 10,000 people	.278[a]	.100	1.32
Urbanization			
(Less than 6% urban)			
At least 6% urban	−.390[a]	.106	0.68
Female employment			
(Less than 5.5% of female			
population employed			
in the modern sector)			
At least 5.5% of female			
population employed			
in the modern sector	.097	.126	1.10

NOTES: Reference category in parentheses; $\chi^2(16) = 470.56$; pseudo $R^2 = .1174$; pseudo $R^2 = (L_0-L_m)/L_0$, where L_0 is the value of the likelihood-ratio χ^2 statistic for the model with intercept only, and L_m is the value for the model in which other variables have been included.

[a]$p \leq .01$ (two-tailed test).

unexpected and may reflect several methodological problems in measuring accessibility in this way. The nearest SDP may provide poor-quality services and, thus, may not be the clinic the woman would use. Moreover, women may choose to travel to a source that is not in their immediate surroundings to ensure that their use of contraception is kept private (Committee on Population, 1991).

District rural literacy and whether the woman's household had electricity are second only to number of family planning SDPs in having strong positive associations with contraceptive use. Women who lived in districts where at least 50 percent of the rural population was literate were more than 2.5 times as likely to use contraception than women who lived in rural areas with lower levels of literacy, regardless of their own educational attainment. There is also an individual-level education effect. Women with one to 6 years of schooling were more likely to use contraception than women with no schooling. Women with more than 7 years of education were even more likely to do so. Njogu (1991), in a study of the individual-level factors related to contraceptive use, also showed that educational level was strongly associated with contraceptive use in the KDHS and KFS.

With regard to household electricity, a woman living in an electrified home was more than 2.5 times as likely to use contraception than a woman living in a house without electricity. This variable is probably a reflection of level of household income. Another income-related variable, household flooring, also has a significant association with contraception.

Several variables that are generally associated with exposure to modern ideas and values show a positive effect on contraceptive use. A woman who belongs to a women's group, listens to the radio at least once a week, or lives in a district with at least 25 kilometers of paved road per 10,000 people is significantly more likely to use contraception than a woman without one or more of these characteristics. Similar results were found in a study by Hammerslough (1991b) in which he used community-level data from the Kenya Community Survey and KDHS individual-level survey data to test the association between membership in a women's group and contraceptive use. Focus group discussions, reported in this same study, indicated that women's groups served as an interface between their members and modern sector organizations. It is suggested that this relationship fosters contact with family planning associations, as well as providing support for using contraception.

It is often postulated that increased urbanization also exposes women to modern values and institutions, and thus should have a positive association with contraceptive use. In this analysis, both measures of urbanization— whether the woman lives in an urban or rural area, and whether she lives in a district that is more than 6 percent urban—have significant *negative* effects on contraceptive use. It may be that once factors associated with urban residence, such as income level, accessibility to family planning services, and modernization indicators, are controlled, there is nothing about urbanization itself that is significant in increasing contraceptive use and in fact it can be a negative influence. Another explanation may be that in Kenya the distinction between urban and rural residents is often ambiguous. There is significant movement of people back and forth between rural and urban areas, with people often maintaining close ties to their rural communities rather than developing permanent ties in the urban area where they have gone to work. In such a case, the urban-rural dichotomy, with people living in urban areas having different and "more modern" values than people in rural areas, may not hold.

The percentage of the female population employed in the modern sector of each district was also tested for its relationship to individual contraceptive use. As with urbanization, it was expected that women living in a district with more women employed in the modern sector would be exposed to different values and institutions, as well as there being a trade-off between raising children and working outside the home. Living in a district with at least 5.5 percent of the female population employed in the modern sector did not have a significant relationship to contraceptive use. However, this factor was the most significant variable in determining whether a contraceptor used a modern or traditional method. (The results from this logistic regression are not shown.) Female employment was also the most significant factor in determining whether a woman would use a modern contraceptive versus no contraceptive (results also not shown).

Finally, the effects of two other individual-level variables were tested: age and religion. Women age 25 years and older are more likely to use contraception than younger women. But the estimated probabilities of use for age groups 25-39 and 40 or over did not differ significantly from each other: Women in both groups were more likely to use contraception than women age 15-24, but women age 25-39 were not more likely to use contraception than women age 40 or more, and vice versa. This finding is consistent with the results in Chapter 4, which indicate that fertility declines occurred in both middle and later age groups.

Religion is not significantly associated with contraceptive use. This finding is not unexpected, given the steep fertility declines during the 1980s in the Coast Province, an area that is largely Muslim (see Chapter 4).

Other variables not measured in this model that could affect contraceptive use are cultural norms valuing high fertility and child mortality. A contraceptive prevalence differentials study (Population Studies and Research Institute, 1991) of six districts conducted in 1990 noted that these two factors were associated with areas of low to medium contraceptive prevalence. Survey respondents, when asked about the value of children, noted that children provided additional household income as well as psychological satisfaction. Women also mentioned the costs of children, indicating that feeding, clothing, and educating children were expensive. In addition, the availability of future economic opportunities, particularly for men, was cited as a concern.

Although many of the variables examined in this multivariate analysis are significant, it is important to note that the model as a whole explains little of the variation in the probability of using contraception. The pseudo R^2 is .12. This result supports our earlier hypothesis in Chapter 4 that the declines in fertility seem to stem from a central force and not necessarily from individuals or regions with particular development or other characteristics. This result is consistent with the weak linkage between fertility and socioeconomic variables at the district level.

SUMMARY

This chapter explores relationships between socioeconomic factors and changes in fertility, mortality, and contraceptive use. The declines in child mortality were strongly associated with female education and adult literacy at the district level. Little relationship was found to the availability of district-level health services.

Examination of associations between the declines in fertility and several socioeconomic factors here and in Chapter 4 revealed very weak relations to education, urbanization, and child mortality. Employment in the modern sector showed a stronger relationship at the district level and was the only developmental indicator that was related to the fertility declines in a significant way.

Multivariate analysis of contraceptive use highlighted the strong relationship between individual-level contraceptive use and the number of family planning service delivery points in a district. Other significant associations were found with district rural literacy, individual education, household electricity and type of flooring, district road density, membership in a women's organization, and weekly radio listening. Female employment in the modern sector was the strongest indicator in determining whether a contraceptor used a modern versus a traditional method. Caution must be taken in interpreting the results from these models, however, because only a small part of the variation in individual contraceptive use has been explained.

APPENDIX

Tables 7A-1A and 7A-1B follow on pages 164-167.

TABLE 7A-1A Socioeconomic Indicators for Districts—Education and Employment Indices

	Education		Employment	
Province and District	Women Age 15-44 with No Schooling, 1979 (%)	Adults Literate, 1981-1988[a] (%)	Index of Female Employment in Modern Sector, 1980[b] (%)	Index of Male Employment in Modern Sector, 1980[c] (%)
Nairobi	17.4		52.0	109.1
Central				
Kiambu	24.3	71	23.3	40.2
Kirinyaga	36.9	61	12.8	14.9
Muranga	26.8	66	11.7	22.9
Nyandarua	33.4	65	11.6	20.4
Nyeri	19.7	68	14.7	21.5
Coast				
Kilifi	84.9	32	6.1	17.0
Kwale	82.1	46	4.3	17.8
Lamu	75.1		5.0	24.2
Mombasa	40.5		31.9	81.1
Taita Taveta	38.1	60	11.6	43.5
Tana River	84.3		4.1	12.1
Eastern				
Embu	38.4	51	7.0	17.5
Isiolo	84.7		12.5	18.5
Kitui	64.2	51	3.3	9.3
Machakos	31.1	56	5.4	14.6
Marsabit	94.3		3.2	10.6
Meru	46.5	50	5.9	12.1
Northeastern				
Garissa	95.4		1.4	8.6
Mandera	97.7		0.4	4.5
Wajir	97.4		0.4	3.8

	^{a}		^{b}	^{c}
Nyanza				
Kisii	38.5	47	3.8	10.8
Kisumu	35.7	49	11.8	30.2
Siaya	49.9	44	2.2	6.8
South Nyanza	49.6	39	3.4	8.1
Rift Valley				
Baringo	59.9	38	8.6	14.0
Elgeyo Marakwet	49.7	36	5.0	8.8
Kajiado	70.8	25	7.8	12.5
Kericho	49.0	46	11.7	40.1
Laikipia	45.4	46	20.4	40.4
Nakuru	38.8	52	22.3	48.5
Nandi	42.2	48	10.7	34.4
Narok	83.7	30	3.5	8.1
Samburu	91.9		2.6	20.3
Trans Nzoia	47.8	52	16.4	30.6
Turkana	96.3		0.6	4.6
Uasin Gishu	41.4	54	23.4	36.8
West Pokot	88.0	42	2.8	6.6
Western				
Bungoma	35.3	52	4.8	11.3
Busia	56.0	42	6.0	7.9
Kakamega	40.3	51	5.3	16.4

^{a} Percentage of adults (both sexes) literate: average of 1981 and 1988 surveys.

^{b} Percentage of female employment in the modern sector, 1980: numbers of women employed in modern sector from 1980 employment survey dividied by women aged 15-44 years at 1979 census.

^{c} Percentage of male employment in the modern sector, 1980: numbers of men employed in modern sectcr from 1980 employmnet survey divided by men aged 15-44 years at 1979 census.

TABLE 7A-1B Socioeconomic Indicators for Districts—Population Density, Health, and Economic Indices

Province and District	Health					Economic
	Population Density, 1979 (per km^2)	Outpatients with Malaria, 1976-1984 (%)	Children Wasted, 1982[a] (%)	Children Stunted, 1982[b] (%)	Index of Health Facilities[c]	Households with No Piped Water, 1982 (%)
Nairobi	1,210					
Central						
Kiambu	280	6.5	1.2	17.5	577	75.0
Kirinyaga	202	7.9	1.9	24.5	329	77.4
Muranga	261	12.9	4.2	24.8	623	76.2
Nyandarua	66	3.6	2.0	12.4	490	82.4
Nyeri	148	5.4	3.0	18.5	525	78.6
Coast						
Kilifi	34	25.4	5.1	42.1	1,203	74.7
Kwale	34	24.6	4.9	38.5	1,035	86.0
Lamu	6	20.2	5.1	42.1	240	74.7
Mombasa	1,622	23.4			178	
Taita Taveta	8	28.6	4.7	14.7	648	80.5
Tana River	2	28.6	5.1	42.1	905	74.7
Eastern						
Embu	96	21.8	2.0	22.3	504	89.1
Isiolo	1	24.4			436	
Kitui	15	24.5	1.8	30.0	1,974	100.0
Machakos	72	21.3	2.9	23.1	1,526	95.3
Marsabit	1	17.0			2,023	
Meru	83	18.1	3.3	16.8	1,265	68.4
Northeastern						
Garissa	2	21.1			2,069	
Mandera	3	24.3			4,151	
Wajir	2	20.6			2,860	

Nyanza					
Kisii	395	32.3	5.0	33.1	650	99.0
Kisumu	230	30.9	3.4	19.8	482	87.5
Siaya	188	29.7	6.3	36.6	711	98.1
South Nyanza	143	32.2	1.5	25.3	973	99.5
Rift Valley					
Baringo	20	10.9	6.4	19.4	566	93.0
Elgeyo Marakwet	65	12.7	2.1	18.6	179	98.1
Kajiado	7	16.5	2.5	19.8	699	93.2
Kericho	161	17.5	3.0	18.1	435	85.7
Laikipia	13	9.4	6.4	19.4	617	93.0
Nakuru	90	9.6	2.3	34.5	832	85.8
Nandi	109	22.8	3.3	12.1	364	79.6
Narok	13	15.0	2.5	19.8	842	93.2
Samburu	4	16.9			784	
Trans Nzoia	124	20.1	2.8	19.1	645	86.8
Turkana	2	19.7			904	
Uasin Gishu	89	19.3	2.7	17.8	412	95.2
West Pokot	17	24.8	2.1	18.6	671	98.1
Western					
Bungoma	163	38.5	2.0	24.7	1,042	89.3
Busia	183	31.6	2.1	21.1	658	99.3
Kakamega	294	33.0	2.0	26.7	1,489	96.5

[a] Percentage of children wasted (i.e., low height for age): less than 80% of WHO standard (1982 Nutrition Survey).

[b] Percentage of children stunted (i.e., low weight for height): less than 90% of WHO standard (1982 Nutrition Survey).

[c] Index of health facilities: persons per health facility (hospitals, health centers, clinics, and dispensaries) multiplied by the square root of the land area.

8

Conclusions

It is not possible to derive irrefutable conclusions about the determinants of demographic change from an analysis of data for any one country. Many factors are operating simultaneously with multiple interactions. Variations among social and regional population subaggregates contribute significant information, but it must not be forgotten that some of the major influences are likely to be common to all of them. These difficulties exist even when there is an abundance of reliable data, which is by no means true for Kenya. Probably the biggest handicap for the present purpose has been the limitation of quantitative measures for subaggregates of the population. For example, only crude and sketchy estimates of adult mortality and of migration can be derived for districts, so there is a considerable barrier to any study of the components of population growth.[1] Even basic indices that are known with fair precision at the national level, such as the total fertility and child mortality rates, can only be estimated roughly for units smaller than provinces. This limitation is a consequence of the comparatively small sample sizes in the household surveys that provide the most satisfactory detailed data. Similar conditions apply to the social and economic indicators whose links with demographic change are explored. The extent to which residents in rural areas participate in the activities and services of the main urban centers, such as Nairobi, Mombasa, and Kisumu, is hard to assess.

---

[1]This report does not examine recent migration patterns due to very limited access to data from the 1989 census.

For all the reasons given, attempts to seek explanations for the significant changes in the demography of Kenya must be an assessment of consistencies. How far do the particular features of the country fit in with general theories and findings of demographic transition as deduced from world experience? The nature of the specific evidence gives more power to negative results than to positive ones. A contradiction has a validity on its own that may be argued away on the grounds of inadequate data or peculiar conditions but nevertheless must be recognized. A conformity is of much less weight because it is normally one that fits with many alternative interpretations.

The trends in child mortality and fertility have completely different characteristics, with the former being a continuous decline over several decades and the latter a very recent fall. This finding does not prove that they have no major causes in common but demonstrates that, if they do, the causes operate in distinctly separate ways. It is legitimate therefore to examine the two phenomena independently before raising questions about interactions. The limited and uncertain information on adult mortality makes it impracticable to study this component separately. However, it can be noted that there was a substantial decrease in adult mortality from the 1950s, although the bits and pieces of indirect evidence are inadequate to measure its size with any confidence. The moderate correlation between the levels of child and adult mortality by districts in the period 1969-1979 engenders confidence in the measures, because the two sets were derived by methods that were largely independent. There is then a plausible argument for the claim that trends in child and adult mortality from the 1950s to the 1970s were similar, although the materials are not sufficient to detect any variations in time and regional patterns that might contribute to the elucidation of determinants.

MORTALITY

The continuance of the mortality change from the earlier periods and the small accretion of new data at the subaggregate level mean that there is little more to add to the thorough examinations in previous studies. The only novelty in this report is the greater concentration on trends. The steady declines in child mortality from the 1950s have been examined in Chapter 3. Despite the data problems for the most recent period, it is fair to deduce that the improvement in the 1980s was at an even faster pace than in the 1960s and 1970s. It might seem surprising that the unfavorable economic experience of the later period, relative to the earlier, cannot be detected in the child mortality record (see Working Group on Demographic Effects of Economic and Social Reversals, 1993, for an examination of the issue).

The cross-sectional analyses of district variations in child mortality found a number of associations that can broadly be described as environmental. These were with the incidence of malaria, the malnutrition measures of stunting and wasting, and ecological zones. In this classification, cultural factors are included with environmental because there is essentially no separation of the ecological effects from those due to the behavior of the communities living in the district units. In particular, the very high childhood mortality on the margins of Lake Victoria can be ascribed to diseases such as malaria or to the practices of tribal groups, particularly the Luo. Because there was no significant alteration in these "environmental" conditions over the period examined, they would not be expected to appear prominently as associated with trends. That turns out to be so and simplifies the consideration of what may be called "developmental" factors.

The social and economic advances of the country as a whole since independence in 1963 are outlined in Chapter 2. In light of the impressive progress, the strong improvement in child mortality is no surprise. But the overall gains provide no opportunities for a better understanding of the specific factors that were the most important. The large variations in child mortality trends among districts do present such opportunities. The variable that emerges as clearly significant for lower mortality is a higher standard of education. The level of education can be measured in a number of ways. Several alternative specifications were explored that showed very similar resulting associations with the trends in child mortality. The simplest is the proportion of adult women with no schooling, which has been adopted here to demonstrate the quantitative relations with trends in $_5q_0$, the proportion of children dying by age 5 years. The correlation is strong and consistent, except for a few outlying observations for the more remote areas, where there are doubts about the accuracy of the measures of the mortality trend. The association between child mortality trends and adult literacy proportions is almost equally impressive, despite some reservations about the validity of the latter estimates. It is also relevant to note here that adult mortality in 1969-1979 is correlated with the education level of the women over districts.

Differentials in child mortality by education of the mother have been a focus of interest since at least the studies of Caldwell (1979) and Behm (1979). The large size and near universality of the effects are well established, but the mechanisms by which they arise are still controversial. It is generally thought that well-educated women tend to be wealthier, to reside in better houses and environments, and to be less constrained in decisions about their children's welfare. In Chapter 3, the $_5q_0$ values by the education of the mother as calculated from the Kenya Fertility Survey (KFS) and the Kenya Demographic and Health Survey (KDHS) data are shown. In both surveys, child mortality for women with no schooling was about twice that of women in the highest education group with more than 9 years of school. But the reduction in child mortality between the surveys was much the same for all schooling categories. In particular, the decline for women with no schooling was nearly identical with the improvement for Kenya as a whole, despite the residual nature of the group due to the rapid advance of female education. Only a small fraction of the child mortality reduction was a consequence of the changing composition of women by grade of schooling. The indications are that the same features were present in earlier child mortality improvements.

The configuration of these results for individuals and district aggregates does not support the view that the driving force in the child mortality trends is the specific benefit at the family level of an educated mother. Individual education may be and probably is significant for the existence and preservation of differentials at points in time, although there may be confounding with other social and economic determinants. The strong reduction in child mortality for the offspring of women with no schooling demonstrates that more general influences are operating. At the district aggregations, the similarity of the associations of child mortality trends with female education and adult literacy (both sexes), as well as the adult mortality correlation with female education, again suggest general rather than specific forces.

In sum, what is notable is the extension of child mortality declines to mothers with little schooling if the educational achievement of the district is good. Taken together, the relationships suggest that the underlying determinant of the child mortality reductions is the increase in knowledge related to the capacity of the family to control its own environment. Obviously formal education is an important component, but improvements in child care tend to spread over a community even if they begin in only limited sections of it. The apparent lack of much association at the district level between child mortality trends and health indicators, particularly health facilities, is disappointing. Although the measures of the latter are crude, they should be enough to give a rough guide to the opportunities for child care. But any relation may be lost among other influences.

FERTILITY

The fertility decline of 20 percent in a decade occurred sharply, following 20 years of high and probably slightly rising fertility rates (Chapter 4). The decline was primarily a consequence of the increased use of contraception to control births (Chapter 5). The effect extended to every province of the country, except possibly the remote Northeastern Province for which there is no information. Although the size of the decline varied by regions, it was substantial in widely spaced districts. The simultaneous initiation of the downward trend in nearly every area strongly suggests that the determinants contained a powerful central component. There are no signs of a gradual spread from the more favored or developed regions to the less advanced. Indeed the linkages by district of the fertility reductions with the developmental indicators of education, urbanization, mortality, and population density are extremely weak. It is true that the quantitative relations of these to the fertility declines can be analyzed only for 17 of the 41 districts because of data limitations. The excluded areas contain all the remote districts with poor development and, possibly, little fertility decline, although this is not known with certainty. However, the restriction of the units to the more populous districts does not detract from the evidence they provide. Of particular note are the districts of the Coast Province for which the fertility decline was 27 percent, second only to Central Province. A greater part of Coast's decline compared to other regions may have been due to later ages at first birth, but the contraceptive component was also considerable. Yet, apart from Northeastern Province, the Coast had the lowest values of development indices for education, literacy, and child mortality improvements.

Further insights into the nature of the fertility transition come from the analysis of the trends in parity progression ratios by cohorts, calculated from the KDHS birth histories. The striking feature of the pattern is the similarity of the trends in size and timing at all birth orders. It appears that the pressures toward birth limitation had their impact on parents of different ages and family sizes at the same time. The gradual spread of birth limitation from the middle parities to the higher and then to the lower orders, typical in the early stages of fertility transition in Latin America and Asia, does not hold in Kenya.

The only socioeconomic indicator having a possible association with fertility declines by district is employment in the modern sector. It is clear that some employees in the towns, particularly Nairobi, Mombasa, and Kisumu, reside in surrounding rural areas. Their transference to the districts of residence would decrease fertility and raise modern sector employment. How large the changes would be is hard to guess, but they might shift a rather uncertain correlation to an impressive one. The associations are much the same for female and male employment. It cannot then be claimed that any effects operate through the mothers rather than the fathers, although such a mechanism cannot be rejected.

Although the observations on fertility declines by district are too restricted and unreliable to support a valid multivariate analysis of the linked factors, much can be gained by investigation of the contraceptive data from the KDHS. It has been established in Chapter 5 that increased use of contraception is closely tracked by fertility reductions. Because contraceptive use was so low at the KFS, with the partial exception of a few subcategories, the multivariate analysis of the KDHS reports of contraception by individuals can serve as an effective surrogate for a direct examination of usage trends. This analysis is presented in Chapter 7.

The proportion of the variation in contraceptive use contributed by the independent variables is small—a result that is consistent with the failure to find much linkage in the crude district comparisons. Nevertheless, the exercise yielded several interesting results. Some of these are negative, notably the lack of differences by religion, in spite of the claims that Muslims, mainly in Coast Province, would be more resistant to the spread of family planning. The small differences in use of contraceptives by age of women from 25 years on fits with evidence from the parity progression ratios.

The significance of educational attainment at the individual level and the rural literacy rate at the district level may appear to contradict the comments above on the weakness of the links between developmental indicators and fertility declines. This is not necessarily the case, however, because contraceptive use by the better-educated women at the KFS was far from negligible. Here, there is a distinction between fertility trends and cross-sectional differences at points of time.

There is a cluster of variables that have significant relations with contraceptive use and that might be indicators of economic standards or of openness to external influences. These are the presence of electricity, a house floor other than mud, and a habit of radio listening at the household level. Participation in a women's organization is also a factor in contraceptive use.

The sharp fertility transition affecting nearly all regions, educational groups, and birth orders gives weight to the view that the changing social and economic factors for Kenya as a whole, from the late 1970s onward, were a major stimulus to fertility reduction. The three outstanding features of the process were the deterioration in real wages, the rise of living standards, and the growing strength of the family planning program.[2] The economic conditions provided the push, and the programs the opportunity. The key proximate determinant in the fertility declines was the increase in contraception (see Chapter 5). Of course that alone does not prove that the supply of family planning services was a significant element in the expanding usage, compared to the demand for family limitation. Rather, the evidence lies in the vigor with which the provision of services was pursued by the Kenyan government and international agencies as outlined in Chapter 6. No doubt the impressive social and economic developments from the 1950s

---

[2]The two features, the deterioration in real wages and the rise of living standards, would seem to be contradictory. Our point is that due to substantial public-sector investments, the quality of life improved, even as wages declined.

to the 1970s, along with the associated declines in child mortality, established the necessary conditions that made fertility reduction possible. But the configurations of change suggest that the more immediate impulse came from the the economic problems of the 1980s and the vigor of the family planning program.

Interpretation of the association at the district level between fertility declines and employment in the modern sector (Chapter 7) must be very speculative. The data weaknesses preclude a close examination of the characteristics of the relation. It is difficult to see it as operating through direct economic pathways of income. Certainly the developed districts of Central Province tend to rank high for both variables, but there are others with such measures that are not as advanced economically, for example, Kericho and Uasin Gishu. Employment in the modern sector may lead to greater awareness of a broader range of ideas in which family planning is seen as a rational solution to economic pressures. If this is so, there are other possible concomitants that might have a bearing. Thus, the massive expansion of the Kenyan tourist industry has increased the contacts with overseas visitors and the potential for communication of attitudes. It is at least interesting that tourism has its largest impact in the Coast Province where the decline in fertility appears so inconsistent with socioeconomic development. Unfortunately, the data to pursue this hypothesis are lacking. The multivariate analysis of contraceptive usage at the time of the KDHS reveals significant factors that can be interpreted as indicators of greater exposure to family control ideas, but a more direct influence of economic conditions cannot be excluded.

THE FUTURE

What indications for future population dynamics come from the analysis of past and current trends? Any such forecasts must assume a reasonable degree of political and economic stability. The histories of Uganda, Mozambique, and Ethiopia show how precarious such an assumption may be in sub-Saharan Africa. The mortality reductions in Kenya have been well established for some 50 years. They will continue in the absence of major catastrophe, such as a dramatic increase in AIDS.[3] The pace of mortality improvement may well slacken due to slower social and economic progress, especially because very low death rates require multiplied effort. The experience of other countries suggests, however, that the momentum built up has yet to expend itself.

---

[3]The more recent data on mortality are unfortunately unreliable and uncertain; it is not possible to separate the possible effects of AIDS from other influences.

In some respects the assessment of the prospects for fertility is more uncertain; in others, more secure. If deteriorating economic conditions were a factor in the initiation of fertility declines, it might be that a reversal in the deterioration would push birth rates up.[4] The acceptance of family planning, once securely established, does not seem to be easily reversible. It has been demonstrated that the rise in contraception is remarkably widely spread by region, social condition, age of women, and family size. The process has not been one of gradual diffusion. As in the case of the mortality trend, the internal momentum should carry it forward toward the substantially lower fertility consistent with desired family sizes. The ideal family size reported at the time of the KFS was 6.2 children, and at the Kenya Contraceptive Prevalence Survey, 5.8. Between those surveys from 1978 to 1984, the level of contraceptive use was much too low to achieve these stated ideals, but a large increase in usage followed. At the time of the KDHS in 1988-1989, the ideal family size had fallen to 4.4 children. It seems reasonable to expect a considerable move toward attaining this ideal in the next decade. Whether there is some intermediate plateau short of replacement levels where the trend would stop (as has happened in other countries) cannot be guessed.

RELATIONSHIP TO DEMOGRAPHIC CHANGE IN OTHER COUNTRIES

This report is a case study of Kenya. Detailed investigations of the patterns of demographic change in other countries of sub-Saharan Africa are outside its scope. Indeed the demographic data sources are much more restricted elsewhere. However, it seemed relevant for comparative purposes to produce estimates of the trends in parity progression ratios over cohorts for countries of Latin America, Asia, and Africa. The striking finding was that the Kenyan pattern presented similar reductions in size and timing across all birth orders, as contrasted with the pattern of Latin America and Asia, where declines spread from the middle parities. However, the pattern in Zimbabwe, Botswana, and Nigeria showed features very much like those of Kenya. This finding gives good support to the views that the Kenya transition is not unique but is shared by other countries of sub-Saharan Africa, and that the pattern emerging in sub-Saharan Africa is different from that of other regions.

---

[4]However, the report of the Working Group on Demographic Effects of Economic and Social Reversals (1993) indicates that short-term economic variation had little effect on marriage and first and second births in Kenya from 1962 to 1987. In comparison to other African countries, Kenya's economy is diversified and the economic crisis of the 1970s and 1980s was not grave, so these results are not unexpected.

References

Baker, J., and S. Khasiani
    1992   Induced abortion in Kenya: Case histories. *Studies in Family Planning* 23(1):34-44.

Bates, R.H.
    1989   *Beyond the Miracle of the Market: The Political Economy of Agrarian Development in Kenya.* Cambridge: Cambridge University Press.

Behm, H.
    1979   Socioeconomic determinants of mortality in Latin America. Pp. 139-165 in *Proceedings of the Meeting on Socioeconomic Determinants and Consequences of Mortality.* New York and Geneva: United Nations and World Health Organization.

Berelson, B.
    1977   Paths to fertility reduction: The policy cube. *Family Planning Perspectives* 9(5):214-219.

Bertrand, J.T., N. Mathu, J. Dwyer, M. Thuo, and G. Wambwa
    1989   Attitudes towards voluntary surgical sterilization in four districts of Kenya. *Studies in Family Planning* 20(5):281-288.

Blacker, J.G.C., J. Mukiza-Gapere, M. Kibet, P. Airey, and L. Werner
    1987   Mortality differentials in Kenya. Paper presented to the International Union for the Scientific Study of Population seminar on Mortality and Society in Sub-Saharan Africa, Yaoundé, October 19-23.

Bongaarts, J.
    1982   The fertility-inhibiting effects of the intermediate fertility variables. *Studies in Family Planning* 13(6/7):179-189.

Bongaarts, J., and R.G. Potter
    1983   *Fertility, Biology, and Behavior.* New York: Academic Press.

Bongaarts, J., O. Frank, and R. Lesthaeghe
    1984   The proximate determinants of fertility in sub-Saharan Africa. *Population and Development Review* 10(3):511-537.

176

Brass, W.
  1964   Uses of census or survey data for the estimation of vital rates (E/CN.14/CAS.4/
         V57). Paper prepared for the African Seminar on Vital Statistics, Addis Ababa,
         December 14-19.
  1981   The use of the Gompertz relational model to estimate fertility. Pp. 345-362 in
         International Union for the Scientific Study of Population Conference Volume,
         Vol. 3. Manila. Liège: International Union for the Scientific Study of Popula-
         tion.
  1985   P-F synthesis and parity progression ratios. In *Advances in Methods for Estimat-
         ing Fertility and Mortality from Limited and Defective Data*. London: The Centre
         for Population Studies, London School of Hygiene and Tropical Medicine, Univer-
         sity of London

Brass, W., and K. Hill
  1973   Estimating adult mortality from orphanhood. Pp. 111-123 in *International Popu-
         lation Conference, Liège, 1973*, Vol. 3. Liège: International Union for the
         Scientific Study of Population.

Brass, W., and F. Juarez
  1983   Censored cohort parity progression ratios from birth histories. *Asian and Pacific
         Census Forum* 10(1):5-13.

Caldwell, J.C.
  1979   Education as a factor in mortality decline: An examination of Nigerian data.
         Population Studies 33(3):395-413.

Caldwell, J.C., I.O. Orubuloye, and P. Caldwell
  1992   Fertility decline in Africa: A new type of transition? *Population and Develop-
         ment Review* 18(2):211-242.

Center for International Research
  1991   HIV/AIDS surveillance data base. U.S. Bureau of the Census, Washington, D.C.

Coale, A.J.
  1973   The demographic transition reconsidered. Pp. 60-72 in *International Population
         Conference, Liège, 1973*, Vol. 1. Liège: International Union for the Scientific
         Study of Population.

Cochrane, S.H., and S.M. Farid
  1989   *Fertility in Sub-Saharan Africa*. World Bank Discussion Papers No. 43. Wash-
         ington, D.C.: The World Bank.

Collier, P., and D. Lal
  1980   *Poverty and Growth in Kenya*. World Bank Staff Working Paper No. 389. Wash-
         ington, D.C.: The World Bank.

Committee on Population
  1991   *Measuring the Influence of Accessibility of Family Planning Services in Develop-
         ing Countries: Summary of an Expert Meeting*. Commission on Behavioral and
         Social Sciences and Education, National Research Council. Washington, D.C.:
         National Academy Press.

Court, D., and D. Ghai
  1974   *Education and Development: New Perspectives from Kenya*. Nairobi: Oxford
         University Press.

Easterlin, R.A., and E. Crimmins
  1985   *The Fertility Revolution: A Demand-Supply Analysis*. Chicago: University of
         Chicago Press.

Ewbank, D., R. Henin, and J. Kekovole
  1986   An integration of demographic and epidemiologic research on mortality in Kenya.
         Pp. 33-85 in *Determinants of Mortality Change and Differentials in Developing
         Countries: The Five Country Case Study Project*. New York: United Nations.

Farley, T.M.M., and E.M. Besley
    1988   The prevalence and aetiology of infertility. Pp. 15-30 in *African Population Conference, Dakar 1988*, Vol. 1. Liège: International Union for the Scientific Study of Population.
Feeney, G.
    1988   The use of parity progression models in evaluating family planning programmes. Pp. 7.1.17-7.1.31 in *African Population Conference, Dakar 1988*, Vol. 3. Liège: International Union for the Scientific Study of Population.
Fendel, R.E., and J. Gill
    1970   Establishing family planning services in Kenya. *Public Health Reports* 85(2):131-139.
Forrester, M.W.
    1962   *Kenya Today.* Gravenhage: Mouton and Co.
Frank, O.
    1983   Infertility in sub-Saharan Africa: Estimates and implications. *Population and Development Review* 9(1):137-144.
Frank, O., and G. McNicoll
    1987   An interpretation of fertility and population policy in Kenya. *Population and Development Review* 13(2):209-243.
Hammerslough, C.R.
    1991a   Proximity to contraceptive services and fertility transition in rural Kenya. Pp. 1287-1304 in *Demographic and Health Surveys World Conference Proceedings*, Vol. II. Columbia, Md.: Institute for Resource Development/Macro International, Inc.
    1991b   Women's groups and contraceptive use in rural Kenya. Paper prepared for International Union for the Scientific Study of Population seminar on the Course of Fertility Transition in Sub-Saharan Africa, Harare, Zimbabwe, November 19-22.
Harbeson, J.W.
    1971   Land reform and politics in Kenya, 1954-1970. *Journal of Modern African Studies* 9(2):231-251.
Hazlewood, A.
    1979   *The Economy of Kenya.* London: Oxford University Press.
Henin, R.
    1985   An assessment of Kenya's family planning program, 1975-79. Pp. 245-298 in *Population, Aid and Development, Proceedings of an International Meeting on Aid and Cooperation in the Field of Population and Development, Florence, 1985.* Liège: International Union for the Scientific Study of Population.
    1987   Kenya's Population Program, 1965-1985. Unpublished report, The Population Council, New York.
Henin, R., A. Korten, and L. Werner
    1982   Evaluation of birth histories: A case study of Kenya. *World Fertility Survey Scientific Reports No. 36.* London: International Statistical Institute and World Fertility Survey.
Heyer, J., J.K. Maitha, and W.M. Senga, eds.
    1976   *Agricultural Development in Kenya: An Economic Assessment.* Oxford: Oxford University Press.
Hobcraft, J., and G. Rodriguez
    1980   Methodological issues in life table analysis of birth histories. Paper presented at the Seminar on the Analysis of Maternity Histories (International Union for the Scientific Study of Population, World Fertility Surveys, Contraceptive Prevalence Surveys), London.

Jacobson, J.
    1990   *The Global Politics of Abortion.* World Watch Paper 92. Washington, D.C.: The
             World Resources Institute.
Jolly, C., and J. Gribble
    1993   The proximate determinants of fertility. In K. Foote, K. Hill, and L. Martin, eds.,
             Demographic Change in Sub-Saharan Africa. Panel on the Population Dynamics
             of Sub-Saharan Africa, Committee on Population, National Research Council.
             Washington, D.C.: National Academy Press.
Juarez, F.
    1983   Family formation in Mexico: A study based on maternity histories from a retro-
             spective fertility survey. Ph.D. thesis, University of London.
    1987   Probabilidades censales de agrandamiento de las familias: Niveles y tendencias de
             la fecundidad en la América Latina. *Notas de Poblacion* No. 43, CELADE.
Kelley, A.C., and C. Nobbe
    1990   *Kenya at the Demographic Turning Point? Hypotheses and a Proposed Research
             Agenda.* World Bank Discussion Papers No. 107. Washington: The World Bank.
Kenya
    1975   *Yearbook of Education.* Ministry of Education. Nairobi: The Government Press.
    1978   *The National Integrated Sample Survey Program, Phase I.* Ministry of Planning
             and National Development, Central Bureau of Statistics, Laboratories for Popula-
             tion Statistics. Reprint No. 21. Nairobi.
    1979   *Yearbook of Education.* Ministry of Education. Nairobi: The Government Press.
    1980   *Kenya Fertility Survey, 1977-78 First Report.* Ministry of Planning and Develop-
             ment, Central Bureau of Statistics, Nairobi.
    1983   *Population Projections for Kenya, 1980-2000.* Ministry of Planning and National
             Development, Central Bureau of Statistics, Nairobi.
    1984a   *Sessional Paper No. 4 - Population Policy Guidelines.* Ministry of Home Affairs
             and National Heritage, Office of the Vice President, Nairobi.
    1984b   *Statement of Hon. Mwai Kibaki at International Population Conference, Mexico
             City.* Ministry of Home Affairs and National Heritage, Office of the Vice Presi-
             dent, Nairobi.
    1986   *Kenya Contraceptive Prevalence Survey, 1984, First Report.* Ministry of Planning
             and National Development, Central Bureau of Statistics, Nairobi.
    1987   *The National Population Strategy.* Ministry of Home Affairs and National Heri-
             tage, National Council on Population and Development, Nairobi.
    1988   *Statistical Abstract, 1988.* Ministry of Planning and National Development, Cen-
             tral Bureau of Statistics. Nairobi: The Government Press.
    1989a   *Economics Survey, 1989.* Ministry of Planning and National Development, Central
             Bureau of Statistics. Nairobi: The Government Press.
    1989b   *Impact of Socioeconomic Development on Fertility in Rural Kenya.* Ministry of
             Planning and National Development, Central Bureau of Statistics. Nairobi: The
             Government Press.
    1989c   *National Development Plan for the Period, 1989 to 1993.* Ministry of Planning
             and National Development, Nairobi.
    1989d   Family planning report, annual totals. Ministry of Health, Health Information
             System. Nairobi.
    1990   *Kenya Rural Literacy Survey 1988 Basic Report.* Ministry of Planning and Na-
             tional Development. Nairobi: The Government Press.
    1991a   *Statistical Abstract, 1990.* Ministry of Planning and National Development, Cen-
             tral Bureau of Statistics. Nairobi: The Government Press.

1991b   *Economic Survey 1991*. Ministry of Planning and National Development, Central
         Bureau of Statistics. Nairobi: The Government Press.
1991c   *Health Information System 1989 Annual Report*. Nairobi: Ministry of Health.
Kenya National Council on Population and Development, and Institute for Resource Development
    1989   *Demographic and Health Survey, 1989*. Columbia, Md.: Institute for Resource
            Development/Macro Systems, Inc.
Kibet, M.K.I.
    1981   Differential mortality in Kenya. Unpublished M.A. thesis, University of Nairobi.
Killick, A., ed.
    1981   *Papers on the Kenyan Economy*. Nairobi: Heinemann Educational Books.
Krystall, A., J.A. Mwaniki, and J.W. Owour
    1978   Kenya. *Studies in Family Planning* 6(8):286-291.
Laing, J.
    1978   Estimating the effects of contraceptive use on fertility. *Studies in Family Plan-
            ning* 9(6):150-175.
Lema, V.M.
    1990   *A Review of Abortion in Kenya*. Nairobi: Centre for the Study of Adolescence.
Lema, V.M., R. Kamau, and K. Rogo
    1989   *Epidemiology of Abortion in Kenya*. Nairobi: Centre for the Study of Adoles-
            cence.
Miller, R.A., L. Ndhlovu, M. Gachara, and A. Fisher
    1991   The situation analysis study of the family planning program in Kenya. *Studies in
            Family Planning* 22(3):131-143.
Nelson, H.D., ed.
    1983   *Kenya, A Country Study*. Washington, D.C.: Foreign Area Studies, American
            University.
Njogu, W.
    1991   Trends and determinants of contraceptive use in Kenya. *Demography* 28(1):83-
            99.
Okoth-Ogendo, H.W.O.
    1981   Land ownership and distribution in Kenya's large farm sector. Chapter VII-4 in
            A. Killick, ed., *Papers on the Kenyan Economy*. Nairobi: Heinemann Educational
            Books.
Oucho, J.O.
    1984   *The Kenyan Land Settlement Programme: Its Demographic and Socio-Economic
            Implications*. Geneva: International Labour Office.
    1987   Formulation, implementation and impact of population policy in Kenya. Chapter
            4 in E. van de Walle and J.A. Ebigbola, eds., *The Cultural Roots of African
            Fertility Regimes*, Proceedings of a Conference. Philadelphia: Population Studies
            Center, University of Pennsylvania.
Panel on Tropical Africa
    1981   Levels and trends of fertility and mortality in Kenya. Unpublished report. Com-
            mittee on Population and Demography, Assembly of Behavioral and Social Sci-
            ences, National Research Council, Washington, D.C.
Parkhurst, F.S., ed.
    1970   *Africa in the Seventies and Eighties*. New York: Praeger and Co.
Phillips, J.F., and K. Kiragu
    1989   The Kenyan National Council for Population and Development: Strategies for
            Improving Organizational Performance. Unpublished consultants report to Kenya
            National Council on Population and Development and USAID on a mission in
            June 1988.

Population Studies and Research Institute
1991   *District Contraceptive Prevalence Differentials Study: A Case Study of Six Districts.* Nairobi: University of Nairobi.

Preston, S., ed.
1977   *Effects of Infant and Child Mortality on Fertility.* New York: Academic Press.

Preston, S., and N. Bennett
1983   A census-based method for estimating adult mortality. *Population Studies* 37:91-
104.

Radel, J.
1973   Kenya's population and family planning policy. In T.E. Smith, ed., *The Politics of
Family Planning in the Third World.* London: Oxford University Press.

Reining, P., F. Camara, B. Chinas, R. Fanale, and S.G. de Millan
1978   *Village Women: Their Changing Lives and Fertility: Studies in Kenya, Mexico
and the Philippines.* Washington, D.C.: American Association for the Advance-
ment of Science.

Rempel, H., and W.J. House
1978   *The Kenya Employment Problem.* Nairobi: Oxford University Press.

Robinson, W.C.
1992   Kenya enters the fertility transition. *Population Studies* 46(4):445-457.

Robinson, W.C., and S.F. Harbison
1993   Components of fertility decline in Kenya: Prospects for the future. *Population
Research Center, Working Paper.* University Park: Pennsylvania State University.

Rogo, K.
1990   Induced abortion in Africa. Paper prepared for the annual meeting of the Population Association of America, Toronto, Canada, May 2-3.

Rutstein, S.O.
1984   *Infant and Child Mortality Levels, Trends and Demographic Differentials.* WFS
Comparative Studies 43. Voorburg, Netherlands: International Statistical Institute.

Saunders, L., and P. Mbiti
1979   *Interagency Maternal and Child Health/Family Planning Information and Education Program—Draft Plan.* Consultants report to the Ministry and Finance and
Planning, Nairobi.

Shapiro, J.
1991   A review of the current literature on internal migration in Kenya. Background
paper prepared for the Working Group on Kenya, Panel on the Population Dynamics of Sub-Saharan Africa, Committee on Population, National Research Council,
Washington, D.C.

Stewart, F.
1976   Kenya's strategy for development. In U.G. Damachi, G. Routh, and A.R.A. Taha,
eds., *Development Paths in Africa and China.* London: Macmillan

Sudan Department of Statistics and Institute for Resource Development
1991   *Sudan Demographic and Health Survey, 1989/1990.* Columbia, Md.: Institute for
Resource Development/Macro International, Inc.

Timæus, I.
1986   An assessment of methods for estimating adult mortality from two sets of data on
maternal orphanhood. *Demography* 23:435-449.
1993   Adult mortality. In K. Foote, K. Hill, and L. Martin, eds., *Demographic Change
in Sub-Saharan Africa.* Panel on Population Dynamics of Sub-Saharan Africa,
Committee on Population, National Research Council. Washington, D.C.: National Academy Press.

United Nations
    1982   *Model Life Tables for Developing Countries. Population Studies 77.* New York: United Nations.
    1983   *Manual X: Indirect Techniques for Demographic Estimation.* New York: United Nations.
United Nations Fund for Population Activities
    1979   *Report of Kenya Needs Assessment Mission.* New York: United Nations Fund for Population Activities.
van de Walle, E.
    1993   Recent trends in marriage ages. In K. Foote, K. Hill, and L. Martin, eds., *Demographic Change in Sub-Saharan Africa.* Panel on Population Dynamics of Sub-Saharan Africa, Committee on Population, National Research Council. Washington, D.C.: National Academy Press.
van de Walle, E., and J.A. Ebigbola
    1987   *The Cultural Roots of African Fertility Regimes.* Proceedings of a Conference. Philadelphia: Population Studies Center, University of Pennsylvania.
van de Walle, E., and F. van de Walle
    1988   Postpartum sexual abstinence in tropical Africa. Paper presented at the International Union for the Scientific Study of Population Seminar on the Biomedical and Demographic Determinants of Human Reproduction, Johns Hopkins University, Baltimore, Md.
Westoff, C.F.
    1991a   Age at marriage, age at first birth, and fertility in Africa. Unpublished manuscript. Princeton University, Princeton, N.J.
    1991b   Reproductive preferences. *Demographic and Health Surveys Comparative Studies 3.* Columbia, Md.: Institute for Resource Development/Macro International, Inc.
Westoff, C.F., and L.H Ochoa
    1991   Unmet need and the demand for family planning. *Demographic and Health Surveys, Comparative Studies 5.* Columbia, Md.: Institute for Resource Development/Macro International, Inc.
Whiting, B.
    1977   Changing life styles in Kenya. *Daedalus* Spring:211-225.
Wilson, C., and J. Cleland
    1987   Demand theories of the fertility transition. *Population Studies* 41(1):5-30.
Working Group on the Demographic Effects of Economic and Social Reversals
    1993   *Demographic Effects of Economic Reversals in Sub-Saharan Africa.* Panel on the Population Dynamics of Sub-Saharan Africa, Committee on Population, National Research Council. Washington, D.C.: National Academy Press.
Working Group on the Effects of Child Survival and General Health Programs on Mortality
    1993   *Effects of Health Programs on Child Mortality in Sub-Saharan Africa.* D. Ewbank and J.N. Gribble, eds. Panel on the Population Dynamics of Sub-Saharan Africa, Committee on Population, National Research Council. Washington, D.C.: National Academy Press.
Working Group on Factors Affecting Contraceptive Use
    1993   *Factors Affecting Contraceptive Use in Sub-Saharan Africa.* Panel on the Population Dynamics of Sub-Saharan Africa, Committee on Population, National Research Council. Washington, D.C.: National Academy Press.
World Bank
    1963   *The Economic Development of Kenya.* Baltimore, Md: The Johns Hopkins University Press.

1975   *Kenya: Into the Second Decade.* Baltimore, Md: The Johns Hopkins University Press.
1980   *Kenya: Population and Development.* Washington, D.C.: The World Bank.
1983   *Kenya: Growth and Structural Change* (two volumes). Washington, D.C.: The World Bank.
1991a   *Kenya: Human Resources—Improving Quality and Access.* Country Operations Division, Eastern African Department. Washington, D.C.: The World Bank.
1991b   *Population and the World Bank: A Review of Activities and Impacts from Eight Case Studies.* Operations Evaluation Department, Report No. 10021. Washington, D.C.
1992   *World Development Report 1992, Development and the Environment, World Development Indicators.* New York: Oxford University Press.